P9-DLZ-421

If you live long enough, and your parents live long enough, you will need this book. You may not need it today, but if you don't, you'll probably need it tomorrow. Julie-Allyson Ieron writes with women in view because more often than not, it falls to the daughters to take care of their aging parents. I found myself drawn into these pages, deeply moved by the weaving together of contemporary stories, excellent research, and compelling biblical truth. For those on the caregiving journey, here is a guide that is practical, compassionate and wise. And it is profoundly Christian. I am glad to recommend it to you.

> —Dr. Ray Pritchard, president, Keep Believing
> Ministries; author, *The Healing Power of Forgiveness*,
> *An Anchor for the Soul, Credo*, and *Why Did This
> Happen to Me?*

Julie Ieron offers practical wisdom for women who want to honor a father or mother in the last years of their lives. Sensitive, compassionate, supportive and down to earth, this book will refresh and sustain caregivers in their quiet ministry that honors Christ and will bring great reward.

> —Colin Smith, senior pastor, Arlington Heights
> Evangelical Free Church

Julie's written a remarkable book that reminds me I'm not alone in my wrestling with how best to honor and care for aging parents. Not only does she unpack this incredibly complex issue from a biblical perspective, but she also provides practical advice for navigating the emotional landmines and medical and financial considerations inherent in this life stage. As I embark on this journey with my own family, I'm glad to know there's a resource to enlighten and encourage me.

> —Jane Johnson Struck, former editor, *Today's
> Christian Woman;* executive editor, *MOMSense*
> magazine

Caregiving is the fast track to burnout, especially for women who already grapple with overcommitment, perfectionism, or stress. But it doesn't have to be that way! In this profoundly practical book, Julie-Allyson Ieron offers sensible steps to keep burnout at bay and shares empathetic "in the trenches with you" encouragement and holistic help with a biblical viewpoint. No matter where you are in the caregiving cycle—seeing its approach, striving midstream, or sapped in the aftermath—you will find that parental caregiving isn't something to fear and endure, but to face and even enjoy. This indispensable book shows you how.

    —Debi Stack, speaker and author of *Martha to the Max: Balanced Living for Perfectionists* and *Smotherly Love: I Know Where Your Buttons Are and I'm Not Afraid to Push Them*

The Overwhelmed Woman's Guide to

Caring for Aging Parents

Julie-Allyson Ieron

MOODY PUBLISHERS

CHICAGO

© 2008 by
JULIE-ALLYSON IERON

All rights reserved. No part of this book may be reproduced in any form without permission in writing from the publisher, except in the case of brief quotations embodied in critical articles or reviews.

All Scripture quotations, unless otherwise indicated, are taken from the *Holy Bible, New International Version.*® NIV.® Copyright © 1973, 1978, 1984 by International Bible Society. Used by permission of Zondervan. All rights reserved.

Scripture quotations marked NLT are taken from the *Holy Bible, New Living Translation,* copyright © 1996, 2004. Used by permission of Tyndale House Publishers, Inc., Wheaton Illinois 60189, U.S.A. All rights reserved.

Scripture quotations marked NKJV are taken from the *New King James Version.* Copyright © 1982 by Thomas Nelson, Inc. Used by permission. All rights reserved.

Scripture quotations marked KJV are taken from the King James Version.

Scriptures quotations marked NCV are from the *Holy Bible, New Century Version,* copyright © 1987, 1988, 1991 by Word Publishing, Nashville, TN 37214. Used by permission.

Scripture quotations marked HCSB are taken from *The Holman Christian Standard Bible,* ®Copyright © 1999, 2000, 2002, 2003 by Holman Bible Publishers. Used by permission. Holman Christian Standard Bible®, Holman CSB®, and HCSB® are federally registered trademarks of Holman Bible Publishers.

All websites and phone numbers listed herein are accurate at the time of publication but may change in the future or cease to exist. The listing of website references and resources does not imply publisher endorsement of the site's entire contents. Groups and organizations are listed for informational purposes, and listing does not imply publisher endorsement of their activities.

Editor: Pam Pugh
Interior Design: Ragont Design
Cover Design: LeVan Fisher Design
Cover Image: Photo © Russell Underwood/Corbis

Library of Congress Cataloging-in-Publication Data

Ieron, Julie-Allyson.
      The overwhelmed woman's guide to— caring for aging parents / Julie-Allyson Ieron.
          p. cm.
      Includes bibliographical references.
      ISBN-13: 978-0-8024-5281-8
      ISBN-10: 0-8024-5281-7
Aging parents—Care—United States. 2. Adult children of aging
      parents—Family relationships—United States. I. Title.

      HQ1063.6.I47 2008
      649.8084'60973—dc22

                                                        2008016016

We hope you enjoy this book from Moody Publishers. Our goal is to provide high-quality, thought-provoking books and products that connect truth to your real needs and challenges. For more information on other books and products written and produced from a biblical perspective, go to www.moodypublishers.com or write to:

Moody Publishers
820 N. LaSalle Boulevard
Chicago, IL 60610

1 3 5 7 9 10 8 6 4 2

Printed in the United States of America

DEDICATION

THIS BOOK IS FOR every caregiver who graciously and without reservation shared her (or his) story with me. My prayer is that it will remind every adult child that we're not alone on the caregiving journey. God is with us—and many others are walking parallel roads to ours. In this camaraderie may we each find peace, strength, and comfort.

CONTENTS

ACKNOWLEDGMENTS

I HAVE MORE PEOPLE to thank for their partnership in the preparation of this book than I have pages to list individual names. But please allow me to list just a few:

For the caregivers who shared your stories—you are my inspiration! I am indebted to you for your willingness to open your lives to readers. May you be encouraged by the fact that your candor will be a blessing to countless others.

For my parents—John and Joy—thank you for your gracious permission to share our family life with readers. I love you both more than words can say.

For the publishing team at Moody—this book's birth has been a true co-labor. In particular, I am grateful to Betsey Newenhuyse, who insisted I pursue this project and shepherded it through the publishing maze. To my talented editor Pam Pugh, and the entire marketing team—I am deeply indebted to you for believing in this project and seeing it to completion.

"I thank my God every time I remember you" (Philippians 1:3).

INTRODUCTION

THIS IS A BOOK ABOUT changing roles. It is the combined stories of dozens of grown children and how they learned to recognize and cope with the shift from taker to giver, from child of their parents to caretakers of those people who nurtured them in their early lives.

It is real. Sometimes poignant. Sometimes gut-wrenching. Sometimes messy. Always challenging. Why? No matter how independent our culture conditions us to be—and no matter how much we cultivate and value that independence—we all share one fact: we are someone's child. Our personal independence is challenged by the fact that we all are placed for better or for worse (with little opportunity for parole) into a people group called *family*. Introduce a marriage, and two people groups, two families, draw us into their circles. Sometimes competing. Sometimes demanding. Always requiring emotional energy and personal resolve.

This book is one tool to help you along your family-aging journey. It will help you identify the emotional and spiritual issues you might face, and it will grapple with real-life dilemmas that have engaged the time and energies of other caregiving families—families much like your own.

Each chapter includes real-life stories from contemporary families who've been there. (Because of the sensitive, candid nature of the stories they've shared, I've identified all family caregivers only by fictitious first names of their choosing.)

Each chapter also features biblical examples and insights in laymen's terms from professionals (e.g., in the elder care, financial, and legal professions). Each of these unique viewpoints provides a necessary sliver of wisdom to help us as our parents become more dependent on us for basic physical, emotional, and spiritual needs.

Weaving through the issues of faith we'll address are observations from biblical relationships including those that comprise the book of Ruth—where a daughter-in-law puts herself on the line to care for the not-always-lovable Naomi. Although the culture and time may be foreign to us, this Bible passage is valuable because its principles transcend time to apply to the fast-paced choices we face.

This is a heartfelt topic for me because it hits close to home—a little too close. I'm an only child whose parents are in their sixties and seventies. In addition to the routine medical issues we face together, four years ago I found myself cast in the role of vocal, insistent patient advocate during my father's stint in cardiology intensive care and subsequent stay in a rehab facility. Additionally, I am the daughter of an only child whose ninety-year-old mother was, as I began writing, still "going strong." My grandmother's care fell to my mother, and I helped her shoulder that burden. Then, just a few months into this project, Gram's health took a quick, unexpected turn—and in just a few days, she was in heaven. Mom and I are still working to disperse her estate and finish the work she left behind. All that to say, I'm right there where you are, in the thick of the issues involved in watching two people I dearly love grow older, and another die unexpectedly.

Since you're somewhere along the continuum I'm traveling, I invite you on this journey beside me. Together we'll seek human and heavenly wisdom to equip us to navigate the choppy waters of caring for our elders.

I found a line in a "Helping Yourself" brochure written by Charles A. Corr, Ph.D., to start us off: "Caregivers must avoid becoming overburdened. If you do, you will be unable to take care of your loved one or yourself. . . . The aim should be to do all that we can—not more than we can—to take care of those we love." *Not more than we can! Let's* keep that counsel close as we begin our journey.

Chapter One

GRANDPA
Can't Jump

Helping aging parents face

the truth about their limitations

Alyssa's Dad—On the B-ball Court

It was a sticky summer evening, and my cousin was hosting a cookout. The teens were playing basketball on the driveway as we waited for the coals to cook our dogs and burgers. The women were chatting while setting out plates and salads. Seated on a cluster of deck chairs, the older guys were trading fish stories. Little kids were digging cities in a sandbox and tossing handfuls of dusty grains.

I saw Dad amble away from his group and toward the front drive. I followed at a distance. He stood and watched the teens shoot hoops. Finally, the athlete in him could stand it no longer. He asked for the ball. The guys stared for a minute, then, in deference to his age, tossed it to him gently. He bounced it twice, getting a look of pure joy. I could almost hear his thoughts: I'll show these guys how to really shoot a basket. I was shooting baskets before they could hold a ball.

He crouched his knees, bent his elbow, and anticipated liftoff. Anticipated. But never delivered. No matter how he tried, he couldn't get his feet *to lift a fraction of an inch off the ground—and the rusty spring in his forearm couldn't loft the ball to within two feet of the basket.*

I remember thinking, Well, here's a news flash! Seventy-year-old men with heart issues can't jump. *Then I looked at his face. Where a moment before he'd been, in his mind, a strapping middle-aged man— now he saw himself as aging. You could read it in his eyes. One of the kids patted him on the back as another retrieved the ball and resumed play. I saw him smile weakly. But I felt something inside me sink as I ducked into the shadows so he wouldn't realize I'd seen him.* Daddy's not getting any younger—and now, even he knows it.

DURING CHOIR PRACTICE several weeks ago, we formed prayer circles. Of the six altos in my circle, one requested prayer for her decision to place her mother in long-term care. A second said her mother-in-law is in the midstages of Alzheimer's disease and has moved in with her, her husband, and their teenaged children. Mom and I added our requests for the ongoing care of my ninety-year-old grandmother and for my dad, who is recovering from a year of four surgeries. A fifth commiserated because she (a nurse) had cared for her ailing father in her home for a decade before his death. The sixth, a forty-something wife and mom, sat silently weeping. "I'm listening," she said, "because although I'm not facing this today, I expect to have these issues soon."

Together, we six women prayed for our elder parents' health and welfare. More powerfully, we carried each other to God's throne— seeking for our sisters in faith God's wisdom, strength, and courage. Because as much as the elders are facing painful issues of aging, so we adult children—as primary caregivers—are dealing with our own grieving, denial, or challenges related to our parents' persistent marches into their elder years.

You need no convincing as to the breadth of need for support. You're here, too. Or, at least, you're anticipating a journey to this land. My prayer is that by reading on you'll realize that although you may be the sole caregiver in your home or family setting, you are by no means alone.

God's Hints

Barbara, sister to my fellow alto who moved her mother into long-term care, looks back on her father's later years to realize God was working in small ways to prepare her for challenges that would come with his death and her mother's increasing dependency. Barbara recalls,

On my parents' sixtieth wedding anniversary my sister and I decided to do something special. We went to the church where they worshiped and used the sanctuary for an old-fashioned sing-along, with Dad leading the singing, like old times. My sister was on the organ, and I was videotaping, so we all could relive it later.

I had a hard time finding a location for the camera because of glare from stained glass windows behind the stage. I kept moving from one location to another, always finding that glare a distraction.

When we viewed the tape later, we noticed all the faces were clear—except Dad's. The light from behind him became like a halo, obscuring his face, and giving him an angelic look as he sang.

I didn't want to think about it then, but today that moment gives me a glimpse into eternity—seeing him singing and worshiping, happy and healthy in God's presence. It's something to hold on to. I see it as God graciously preparing me for what He knew would be coming.

As Barbara was soon to learn, we can't change the fact that on our own midlife and aging journeys, we'll come face to face with an eventuality we'd hoped would never arrive: our parents aren't as young as they used to be. Neither are our in-laws. And sooner than any of us thought, we'll need to do something about it.

For Barbara and her sister, *doing something about it* meant being with their father through months of chemotherapy, only to see disease take his life. It meant being available to their mother while she was living in her own home. And it meant taking a phone call that drained all the humor out of the TV commercial catchphrase "I've fallen, and I can't get up." Their mother had fallen in her own home and suffered severe injuries.

Barbara says facing the tough decisions becomes a little easier because she can cling to the hope resulting from her lifetime of faith. Not a crutch or a cop-out, she finds her relationship with God through Jesus Christ—and the assurance that her parents shared the same relationship—to be a lifeline.

Facing What You Don't Want to Face

Like Barbara's videotaping incident and Alyssa's experience with her dad's attempt to launch a basketball, many of us choose to look away when we see signs of aging in our parents. We don't want to embarrass them. We don't want to take away their independence or damage their self-image. We don't want to acknowledge the inevitable regression of change—because by nature we resist change. (Try taking away your parents' driving privileges and see how much *they* resist change.)

Lulling sameness rocks us into a sedated stupor; we relish it. So when aging wheedles into our lives, we ignore or resist or fight it. We've never known a world without our parents, and we don't want to imagine what it would be like. It's an emotional time for parent and child—yet it's an unavoidable life passage.

Over time our parents' needs become harder to ignore. While subtle at first—helping with groceries, shuttling to routine medical visits, running errands to the pharmacy or bank—at a moment's notice they may rocket into emergency medical decisions, financial and legal obligations, personal household disruption, in-patient care, or end-of-life decisions.

Nurse Meghan cared for her mother-in-law in her home for two years, as the elder woman outlived medical forecasts. Meghan cautions that ignoring the issue won't make it go away. She counsels caregivers to face questions head-on. Ask parents their wishes. Talk openly about medical, financial, and legal decisions before they reach a crisis crescendo. (These are issues we'll address in future chapters, to help equip and prepare you for these difficult conversations.)

Meghan also says, "Don't jump ahead too far and worry about every possibility when you see the first signs. God doesn't intend for us to go twenty steps ahead. Remember, Jesus said, 'Don't worry about tomorrow . . . each day has enough trouble of its own.' But He can teach our families wonderful, rich lessons at *this* stage, if we are honest about it with ourselves and our households."

Adjusting to a Shifting Role

As if we needed a little more steam added to our pressure-cooker lives, we may feel ill-equipped (perhaps even ill-inclined) to meet our aging parents' needs for special attention and time-sapping care. U.S. Surgeon General Carmona estimates that "forty-six million Americans are providing uncompensated care for an adult family member or loved one who is chronically ill or disabled, often sacrificing career advancement, personal pleasures and their own health and well-being out of a combined sense of love and duty."[1]

So if the first step along this continuum is to look squarely at what we don't want to face, the second is to acknowledge it's not easy to assume responsibility for another adult—especially one with whom we have a close relationship, one with whom we share a history, one who knows the quickest ways to rile us up.

Meghan says when she was faced with the decision to take her ailing mother-in-law into her home, all her nursing training went "swoop, right out the window. You're never prepared. When it's in your household, in your family, you need as much good counsel, support, and wisdom as someone with no medical training."

Associations and alliances are popping up to assist us in finding whatever skills and information we lack. According to Gail Gibson Hunt, president of the National Alliance for Caregiving, "Timely information and ongoing support are essential to reduce the terrible stress so many caregivers experience." In this age of global information, much of that counsel, wisdom, and support is a few clicks away.

What Does It Mean to Honor?

For the believer in Christ, this season of change in a family carries added weight because of a desire to *honor* our parents. In childhood, *honor* usually meant *obey*. In young adulthood, it meant *respect*. But now as they age, how are we to *honor* them while balancing their needs with our other obligations?

We can take a cue from the verb's synonyms: to prize, to value, to hold precious, to revere. A car enthusiast, when given the opportunity to purchase a classic vehicle in need of repair, will pour thousands of hours (and dollars) into restoring his prized possession. How much more, if we hold our parents as precious (despite their foibles), will we find ways to invest our limited emotional, physical, and financial resources in their care?

Intriguingly, Jesus uses the Greek word for *honor* numerous times during His ministry—sometimes to encourage us to honor our parents (Matthew 19:19), sometimes to encourage us to honor *His* Father (John 5:23), and once to tell us our obedience to Him will cause our heavenly Father to honor us (John 12:26).

Super, you say, *I value my parents because Jesus said to. But this is real life! What if they're not lovable? What if I'm struggling with my issues? What if I don't have the resources to help them?*

Women have asked these questions for generations. When we think God's Word might be out of touch, we can look in its pages and we find examples of real people who, despite their own issues, looked out for the needs of aging relatives—with great reward. Consider the young widow Ruth. In light of our current life issues, let's dissect her story to glean from it challenge and encouragement in our circumstances. We'll revisit it later, but for now let's see if we can discover how it can work in an imperfect world.

Ruth is grieving her husband and brother-in-law; her father-in-law had apparently died some years before. Then her mother-in-law starts talking about a journey to a land where the people didn't care for Moabites. She and her sister-in-law expect to go with Naomi—and both begin the journey. But reality sets in. Naomi sinks into depression, fueled by grief, disappointment, and shame in having wandered outside God's will. Naomi describes herself as bitter and "too old" (Ruth 1:20, 12).

This isn't the best time for anyone to be close to her. Reluctantly, Orpah returns to her parents' home—but Ruth, in a courageous surge of love, stays with the elder woman—to see to her care alone. Both women are so poor that Ruth will have to work tirelessly to glean a few morsels of food left for the destitute. Yet her commitment doesn't waver. In fact, the *Women's Study Bible* notes, "A foundation of purposeful love and the outworking of devoted deeds set Ruth's commitment apart from verbal clichés and the whim of momentary emotions." Ruth spoke boldly of faith and commitment (1:16–17), and spent her energies putting feet to those words.

Hindsight Is 20/20

In these early stages of caregiving, it may be helpful for us to commit to Ruth's pattern, which I call the three C's of caregiving: calmness, comfort, and compassion. From an eternal perspective, these traits will remain after bandages are changed, medications administered, legal matters resolved. We see it in Ruth's words that offer salve to grief-stricken Naomi. She is calm and measured, not rash to acquiesce to the whim of a sorrowing heart. She offers comfort by her companionship. And she is compassionate, not chastising Naomi but offering friendship as a reason to press on despite an uncertain future.

Offering those three C's to our parents and parents-in-law, beginning today and continuing through all the decisions that come, could be the most parent-honoring—and God-honoring—gift we could give. When we look at this season of life in hindsight, we will have nothing to regret.

Adult daughter Ann, whose energetic ninety-one-year-old mother Beatrice lives in a custom-built apartment in the lower level of the house Ann shares with her husband, says, "Mom is a worrier, but I am not. She feels like she would be too big a burden if she were to get sick. But I am not going to let that fear ruin our 'now.' We'll worry later." This well-reasoned choice is giving Ann's family a "now" to remember and celebrate. And it's an approach my family of worriers may try to apply to our situation as we recognize the signs of aging.

Closing **Prayer**

God, my parents are moving too quickly toward the day they'll step out of this world. I want to make these times with them meaningful and rich. I want to do all I can to meet their needs, but I'll need You to equip me. Show me my next step, and keep me willing to serve You by serving them— in calmness, comfort, and compassion.

Take *Action*

1. Initiate a compassionate, honest conversation with your parent(s) about health, wishes, and dreams. Visit websites on caregiving such as: www.strengthforcaring.com or www.medicalnewstoday.com for suggestions on how to initiate this conversation.

2. Locate Bible passages that strengthen your resolve and keep you encouraged.

3. Talk to friends about their experiences in caregiving.

4. Create an informal support network of caregivers (in person or in cyberspace) who are willing to pray for each other.

Chapter Two

SWINGIN'
Seniors

Fostering the independence
of aging parents

Marlee's Mom—Pink-haired Grandma

The one place I'd never have expected to see my eighty-plus-year-old mom was riding on a float in the Fourth of July parade, dressed in a tie-dyed T-shirt that read "recycled grandma." And yet, there she was, sporting a freshly dyed pink coif and playing air guitar; smiling and laughing—the belle of the ball in the middle of her senior-center friends.

Mother was a model wife and caregiver for years, nursing Dad through a long battle with Parkinson's disease. She gave herself away for him twenty-four hours a day for more than a decade. But now that Dad's gone and since Mother has her health, my brother and I were happy when she asked our opinion about selling her townhouse and moving to a new senior apartment complex. We helped her fill out reams of paperwork and enlisted the family to help her move.

The apartment is partially subsidized by the government, so her rent isn't high. But it's a beautiful place where she has a studio apartment on *the third floor of a security building, can come and go as she pleases, and always has someone to socialize with in the TV and game rooms on the first floor. The complex even has a beauty shop and a doctor's office.*

Since she moved in, I can hardly get her on the telephone—she's always downstairs socializing; volunteering at the senior center next door; or going on day trips to the theatre, shopping, or glitzy restaurants. Her big problems last week were what to wear for a costume party and who to sit with at a Mexican dinner party (because too many of her friends wanted her at their tables). On Sweetest Day, she called my daughter and me to ask what we'd gotten from our loves to celebrate. Our answer was nothing (and my daughter is a newlywed). Mom gleefully said she got a yellow rose from a man in the senior complex. Before I could get too indignant, she explained that he bought one for every lady there.

Sometimes I feel like my kids are adults, and now I have a teenaged mother. But Mother has come alive since she moved—and we couldn't be happier for her.

MY MOM WILL BE turning seventy by the time you read this book. But don't you dare call her old. She neither looks nor acts her age; she is a vibrant woman who wears more hats than many of my middle-aged friends. She has been an active caregiver for her mother. She shuttles my dad—her husband of more than fifty years—to surgeries and doctor's appointments, and has bandaged and treated more of his incisions than a triage nurse. Meanwhile, she is my partner in ministry—handling my calendar, chauffeuring me to speaking engagements, proofreading everything that comes out of my office. She plays organ, piano, and keyboard for weddings, church services, and funerals. But don't ask her to have someone help her keep house—she takes pride in handling it herself.

According to critical care nurse Jeanette Giambalvo, my mom's and Marlee's mom's approaches to senior years are practically the norm today. When she began her nursing career more than thirty years ago, people in their sixties and seventies were considered old.

"But today, it's not unusual for me to have a patient who is more than a hundred years old. They may be ninety and still driving (which can be more than a little scary), or a hundred and still riding a bicycle—really, I see it often. They're not just living long, but many are having a high-quality life well into their later decades." In fact, Jeanette herself is still working at the bedsides of patients in the cardiac ward several days a week, although she is in her seventies.

Able and Motivated

In deference to Jeanette's observations—and my own—this chapter won't be about what people over a "certain age" can't—or shouldn't—do. Instead, it will be about respecting their age and celebrating two undeniable facts: 1) their years of experience can equip them to do more things well now than ever before; and 2) they are freer now than ever to spend bonus time pursuing tasks they couldn't make time for when their families were young. As their adult children, we have the power to free them to do what Marlee's mom is doing—relish the joy of well-earned later years spent doing what makes her feel most fulfilled.

Dozens of my friends' senior-citizen fathers could be poster children for that second fact—about using bonus time. They've waited decades to have the luxury they enjoy today of living for their golf games. Where many seniors tout their cholesterol counts or blood pressures, these senior-dads consider their handicaps their most valuable numbers. When they relocate, it's to the southern U.S., where fairways never hide beneath snowy blankets.

You'll see them on the course nearly every business day—clad in hideous plaid slacks, Grandpa shirts, and mismatched baseball caps—teeing off beside business moguls and Tiger Woods wannabes. Scooting around on carts and endangering the resident squirrels, they may not be getting much in exercise benefit, but the emotional dividends are priceless.

Steppin' Out of the Comfort Zone

If, like Marlee's mom and mine, your parent is able and willing to become involved in social activities, local communities offer options for getting out and getting connected. It may take a little arm twisting or cajoling, but seeking those with like interests can be beneficial. Dr. Judy Salerno, deputy director of the National Institutes of Health's National Institute on Aging, cites studies that show that "staying engaged and maintaining good social connections help older people retain cognitive function."[2]

Marlee sees evidence to confirm this study. Before her mother moved into the apartment, she was hard to please. "My daughter or I would take her out shopping or to lunch; after spending several hours together, we'd take Mother home. As we'd drop her off, she'd say something like, 'Now, what am I supposed to do sitting home alone for the rest of the night?' My daughter has a baby and a husband; I have a household to run and a full-time job. We couldn't entertain Mother all the time. So she'd get sad and down." Now, though, as she enjoys her new relationships Marlee's mother doesn't have to sit alone any night—and she seldom chooses to. That's why Marlee is happy on the nights when she can't get her mom on the phone.

As extended family communities, churches offer many opportunities for seniors to get connected. According to Arlene Allen who directs the national women's ministries department of the Assemblies of God, "The church is the perfect place to help meet the needs of all age groups to make sure everyone is cared for." Arlene's department offers specific ministry resources to local churches who are interested in serving senior citizens, including "*Solace*, a ministry designed for meeting the needs of widows [and] . . . *Quiet Place*, a ministry designed to minister to those with Alzheimer's and their caregivers."

Local hospitals, too, offer social and service opportunities for seniors. While my dad was undergoing heart surgery, I picked up our hospital's magazine. Listed under the heading of "Positively Healthy" were activities for seniors that included: community walking clubs, cell phones for seniors, a health fair, angel tree donation opportunities, a Medicare seminar, exercise classes (including an aqua arthritis class), a fashion show, and more.

Another hospital recently placed me on their senior citizen mailing list (no, I'm not there yet, but hey, these activities look like lots of fun—I wish I had the time to enroll!) that describes a trolley tour of a state park, a suspense thriller at a live theater, a day trip to a flea market, a fireside Christmas luncheon, and a polka fest. Not to mention weekly breakfast and supper clubs, bowling teams, sewing, and arts-and-crafts groups. They even get complimentary valet parking. This is the good life, senior style.

Serving Others for the Sake of Christ

More notably, many seniors are using discretionary time for eternally productive purposes. In the mid-1990s, I recall stifling a yawn when I took the assignment from the editor of *The Standard* magazine to interview and report on senior citizen women serving in Baptist mission work beyond retirement age. But it took only a few moments with the first woman, Alma Bjork, for that yawn to morph into awe.

Alma's story reads like an adventure novel. Her husband was under arrest in China for twenty-two months in the late 1940s. His crime? Preaching the gospel. She and their infant child escaped to the U.S. moments before China's Communist revolution closed the country. She lost her hearing due to a staph infection—which kept the family from ministry in Japan and relegated them to home assignment in the U.S. Her husband lost his battle with Lou Gehrig's disease in 1984. But Alma, widowed and almost 100 percent deaf, wasn't ready to quit. She told me, "Ministry is a total-life commitment." She lives out that refrain by coordinating missions education for her church, participating in ministry training in Vietnam and

Thailand, teaching ninth- and tenth-grade Sunday school, volunteering with high school youth in her church, leading cross-cultural women's Bible studies in her neighborhood, and mentoring college students. Alma is doing more despite her handicap and age than most able-bodied people in their twenties and thirties.

Likewise, the other women I interviewed for that article changed my perceptions. I spoke with Evelyn Christensen, who in her late seventies was drawing huge crowds around the globe to hear her speak about her multimillion-selling book *What Happens When Women Pray.*

Then I met Ruby Eliason (nurse and Ph.D. in health development) and Laura Edwards, M.D., career missionaries who spent fifteen winters of their post-retirement years continuing medical mission work in Cameroon. I don't know if the final article was memorable to readers—but I never forgot those four women.

Then in winter 2000 I received a call from the editor, telling me Ruby and Laura had gone home to heaven—when the Land Rover in which they were riding went off a mountainous road in a remote area of Cameroon. The editor invited me to write the magazine's tribute to them. The question I used to open that article still haunts me: "Who will pick up the mantle and continue the work these have begun?"

But the eternal rewards of senior-sainthood don't require lifelong mission work. Sometimes the mission begins and ends at home. Isabelle saw a close-to-home benefit to her mother's vibrant interaction in others' lives. She describes her mother as "a high-energy person who was still driving at eighty-five. I could see that she was aging by her white hair and wrinkles; however, I never viewed her as old. My mother was a great example to our family with the way she always helped her family and neighbors in sickness and times of trouble. She was always there for someone in need." In helping others, Isabelle's mother provided an example for her children and grandchildren.

God's Use of Older Adults

In these elders I see a biblical pattern of godliness worthy of celebration. In the annals of God's interaction with human beings, He frequently chose to use elders whose faith and example had stood the test of time to accomplish His most notable purposes.

God waited until Abraham was a hundred years old and Sarah was chugging along close behind to bring baby Isaac into their lives and begin to fulfill His promise of making the couple parents to a great nation. If they'd ridden bicycles, they would have qualified for nurse Jeanette's elder hall of fame.

Then there was Moses, toiling under his father-in-law's tutelage until age eighty, when God called to him from a burning-but-not-consumed bush and cast upon him the responsibility of leading millions on a forty-year wilderness trek that wasn't for the faint of heart.

In New Testament times God waited until Zechariah and Elizabeth were well past childbearing years to bring them the infant we call John the Baptist. Zechariah the priest was still taking his turn serving in the temple, although Luke calls both him and Elizabeth "well along in years." God's description of this couple is one I'd want to hear Him speak of my parents, although I dare not call *them* well along in years: "Both of them were upright in the sight of God, observing all the Lord's commandments and regulations blamelessly" (Luke 1:6).

Lest we think God only chose to use the saintly, He didn't abandon the weeping and depressed widow Naomi whose husband disobeyed God by taking his household to the foreign land of Moab (Ruth 1). If you fast-forward to the end of Naomi's story (Ruth 4:16), you'll see God had a ministry reserved for her—once He'd brought her through her grief, provided for her welfare, and restored her joy in serving Him.

I've always loved the statement in one of my dad's favorite psalms. While it's not a guarantee, it does bring comfort—that elder years used for God's glory can be a blessing. To the one who dwells in the shelter of the Most High, God says, "I will be with him in trouble, I will deliver him and honor him. With long life will I satisfy him and show him my salvation" (Psalm 91:15–16).

That may be the best definition I know of swingin' senior saints.

Closing **Prayer**

God, thank You for these reminders that You don't disqualify anyone because of age or handicaps. Help me see my aging parents through Your eyes. Let me catch a glimpse of Your perspective on their value, their potential, their continued callings. Help me participate in the joyful living You have yet planned for them. Amen.

Take *Action*

1. Talk with your parents about goals they may yet want to accomplish; then see how you can participate in moving them toward those goals.

2. Encourage your parents to consider ministries that fit their gifts and abilities.

3. Visit your local hospital's website to learn about programs for seniors.

4. Check online for community senior centers or church-based groups where your parents might find social interaction.

Chapter Three

AN APPLE
a Day

"Healthy aging"

isn't an oxymoron

Barbara's Mom—Missionary on a Walker

Mom suffered a fall in her home and injured her back. She was dehydrated, and we realized she hadn't been eating properly. After a hospitalization, a stay in rehab (where Medicare would only let her remain thirty days), and a long-term stay in a nursing home at our expense, we finally were ready to bring her home.

She couldn't move in with one of us, because she couldn't be alone—not even for the hours when my sister, her husband, and I work every day. She made it clear that despite the stairs she wanted to be in her own home.

So, we began interviewing live-in caregivers. We settled on an immigrant girl from Russia. Not only does she do the cooking, cleaning, laundry, and medication dispensing, but they've become true companions. She takes Mom out to sit on the patio when the weather is nice, and they spend lots of time talking.

For years Mom has had a tradition of picking out a Bible verse card from her promise box and reading it before bed. Now, her caregiver has begun asking if she can pick out the card each night. While Mom reads her the Scripture reference from the card, the caregiver goes to the Bible, finds the verse, and reads it aloud. They discuss it as they prepare Mom for bed.

What's so special is that the caregiver couldn't read English when she came to work in Mom's home. But now, through this nightly routine, she's learning to read English by reading the Bible. When she leaves on Saturday evenings for her one day a week off, I always hear her ask Mom, "Will you say a prayer for me, Miss?" So Mom prays a blessing on her.

Although it's difficult for Mom to get out from home, she is able to minister to this girl in the name of Christ, even as she receives ministry from her. In her eighties and leaning heavily on her walker, Mom is demonstrating that you're never too old—or too infirm—to be a healthy witness for Christ.

IN THE LAST CHAPTER we examined how much elder parents can still do. But perhaps your parent is not going to be riding bicycles when he or she is a hundred. Even if your loved one isn't that healthy, there may be elements of healthy living you can help her incorporate into her daily routine.

According to Dr. Judy Salerno of the National Institute on Aging, "Disease and disability are not inevitable consequences of aging." In fact, the medical community has a whole area of research dedicated to the concept of "healthy aging." Dr. Salerno says, "Maintaining good habits and positive attitudes is what we should all be aiming for."[3] We saw evidence of this in the last chapter in the stories of golfing grand-dads, senior missionaries, and Marlee's mother and her pink-haired senior friends.

Other tips from the NIA include such commonsense suggestions as eating a balanced diet, exercising, and maintaining contacts with family and friends.

To add to our understanding of this broadened definition of

healthy, Healthguide's library of illnesses and conditions describes healthy aging by saying, "It's never too early or too late to take the path of healthy aging. If you are feeling well and vital, good self-care helps slow or prevent many age-related problems. If you now have a long-term (chronic) disease or disability or generally feel old and tired, making more healthy choices can have a big impact on how you feel, both physically and mentally. No matter when you start, a healthy lifestyle improves your quality of life and may extend your lifespan."[4]

A Change in Diet and Exercise

According to this definition, even if your parent is battling disease, making healthy life changes can improve his daily life quality. Certainly good nutrition is paramount. When Barbara's mother collapsed, the family discovered that due to a medication she was taking and to her poor eating habits, her body was depleted of vital nutrients. After receiving liquids and proper foods in the hospital, they saw marked improvement in her mental sharpness and her ability to heal.

This is typical for older adults. According to *Healthguide,* "Most vital organs gradually become less efficient with age. . . . The kidneys also become less able to keep your body hydrated. This makes exercise, water intake, and a well-balanced diet increasingly important over time. An active body that gets plenty of oxygen, water, and nutrients is more likely to function efficiently for a longer period of time."[5]

Many hospitals employ nutritionists who can offer recommendations on balancing your parent's diet in light of medical conditions. Each time my father has been hospitalized for cardiac surgery, we've met with a staff dietician to go over his nutritional restrictions. Mom and I have heard the low-fat, low-cholesterol, low-salt (and, according to Dad, low-taste) diet recitation so many times that during one in-patient stint we rattled it off to the wife of his roommate—including our methods of fooling Dad's taste buds into thinking the food we prepare is higher-fat than it actually is. His roommate's wife took notes.

Likewise, hospitalizations tend to lead to discussions about rehabilitation—which can be tied to improving a senior's exercise routine. Our hospital's cardiac rehab center is staffed with professionals who help patients use state-of-the-art workout equipment to rebuild cardiopulmonary strength. And for parents who have had joint replacement, rehab pros help restore range of motion and increase strength in atrophied limbs. But even those who haven't been hospitalized often can (with a doctor's permission) benefit from a gentle, regular workout routine. The NIA offers suggestions and a workout video at http://www.nia/exercisevideo/publications.orgexercisevhs.asp.

A Change in Vantage Point

In addition to diet or exercise, healthy aging can flow out of a change of perspective—a shift from focusing on what a parent can't do to what he can do.

Several years ago, I sat in an audience as the real-life Sue Thomas, whose work as an FBI agent formed the basis for the TV drama *Sue Thomas, FBI*, addressed the crowd. If you've seen the series, you'll remember Sue is hearing impaired, but her ability to read lips made her an invaluable law enforcement agent for the U.S. government.

I was excited to see her in person (although she didn't look like the actress who played her on TV). But I was shocked to learn that she is suffering from a degenerative eye disease that is taking away her sight. Now, to add to her silent world, she is to be imprisoned in a darkened world. But she made the most remarkable affirmation to the crowd: "Soon, I will not be able to see or hear anything from this world. But I have a perfectly clear connection with heaven. I can hear my heavenly Father when He speaks to me—and I can speak to Him. And that's what my ministry will be for as long as He gives me breath. I can pray—and I *will* pray." I'd call that a healthy-living choice.

Author Jennifer Thomas, a Christian psychologist who did her doctoral work on the psychology of aging, suggests that we can help our parents age in a healthier way by encouraging them to find value in things they enjoy and can still do. Dr. Thomas suggests involvement in social settings like exercise groups (check with their medical doctors to be sure the activity level is appropriate for their health and age), church activities, and service projects. She gives the example of stuffing envelopes for a local nonprofit group or folding inserts for the church bulletin. The important thing is that a parent finds value in what he or she is doing—and sees that it will enhance others' lives.

Beatrice is a ninety-one-year-old widow—and she has unknowingly filled Dr. Thomas's prescription. Her daughter Ann explains, "Mom learned to use the Internet for e-mailing, not surfing. Sometimes she asks me to check an attachment before she opens it; otherwise, she does it all herself. She keeps in touch with family and friends this way. She is also active about calling people on the telephone and having nice long talks with them."

Beatrice pipes in to clarify that she adores keeping in touch with her twenty grandchildren and twenty-four great-grandchildren by e-mail. "I am fortunate that my children keep me informed—they call often. It makes living so . . . " Her sparkling eyes and smile evoke several words to finish that statement: *worthwhile, exciting, energizing.*

Beatrice keeps to a vigorous routine. She drives to the beauty shop, the grocery store, and Bible study, and she gets around on her decorative cane faster than many people half her age. She also babysits for her great-grandchildren—including a four-year-old whom she watches for several hours at a time. She credits her agility to her healthy habits: "I walk on the treadmill every day." *Every day?* "Yes, I watch *Jeopardy* and walk a mile while I'm watching."

Although Ann and her husband installed an elevator in the home they built to share with Beatrice (who has her own apartment downstairs), Beatrice faithfully loads it with her groceries or laundry, closes the door, walks down the stairs, and calls the elevator from below to send down the goods. "It's good for my knees if I walk the stairs," she says.

The way Beatrice is rising to the aging challenge is a model for other healthy elders to follow. Dr. Thomas says, "For most of us, self-worth is tied to our professions, our spouses, our children." But when retirement comes, children mature, and a spouse dies, identity gets clouded and the question becomes, "Does my life matter? I encourage families with a relative who has lost some independence to help them maintain an ability to serve others, because that's a critical part of living."

Connectedness with Family Far and Near

Since one key to healthy aging is maintaining social connections, a family's involvement in an aging parent's life can be a great boon to self-worth and value. For example, family members could take turns visiting a parent or taking him out on errands or excursions. When Barbara's mother was getting ready to return home, Barbara and her sister would pick her up and take her home or out to eat or on brief shopping trips before taking her back to the nursing home. These helped convince her that living more independently was a viable option.

But not all families live close enough for frequent face-to-face visits. Colin Smith, author of a book on the Ten Commandments titled *The 10 Greatest Struggles of Your Life*, says,

> What is important is to participate in their lives, at a level appropriate to their need. To do practical things for them and find the most appropriate means in any situation to give them weight. One way is to be in touch regularly, visiting, spending time, telephoning, writing—whatever means of communication works best. Another way is being available to assist with their needs and challenges.

Born in Edinburgh, Scotland, Pastor Colin has a special challenge in giving weight to the needs of his parents. While Colin has pastored in suburban Chicago for more than a decade, his parents and parents-in-law still live in the United Kingdom.

[My wife] Karen and I have a commitment to give our parents time every year. We take a month every year and spend quality time with them. We will probably change the pattern now, having shorter trips a couple of times a year, because their needs are changing.

What has been a blessing to us, despite being four thousand miles away, is meaningful participation in their lives each week. I talk to them every week; in fact, just this morning I spent a half hour on the telephone with my parents.

Then, when we are with them, it is focused time. We aren't in and out of the house on a regular basis, but we find other ways to remain strong in our relationship with them, not only for Karen and me, but also for our sons to remain connected with their grandparents.

Spiritually Healthy Aging

For years, as I've autographed my books at conferences and book signings, I've added the Scripture reference 3 John 2 to my inscription. In the context of this book—and the principle of healthy aging—it seems more apt than ever: "Dear friend, I pray that you may enjoy good health and that all may go well with you, even as your soul is getting along well." Or, as the NLT puts it: "Dear friend, I hope all is well with you and that you are as healthy in body as you are strong in spirit."

In considering healthy aging, it is well to consider habits that increase physical health—but more valuable to consider healthy spiritual aging. Thus our prayer can be that not only the bodies but the souls of our elder loved ones be "strong in spirit" or "get along well."

Barbara's mother demonstrates her spiritual health in that despite limitations, her life is still bearing spiritual fruit. She shows that the aging journey, even at its most challenging, can be the best time to exhibit the fruit of the Spirit: "love, joy, peace, patience, kindness, goodness, faithfulness, gentleness and self-control" (Galatians 5:22–23).

This season may be the time for your parent, especially if he is a person of faith, to consider his lasting legacy—which is less intertwined with a financial portfolio than with the spiritual imprint of his life. Consider David's legacy: "And you, my son Solomon, acknowledge the God of your father, and serve him with wholehearted devotion and with a willing mind, for the Lord searches every heart and understands every motive behind the thoughts. If you seek him, he will be found by you; but if you forsake him, he will reject you forever" (1 Chronicles 28:9). David made mistakes—but in the end his legacy was of one forgiven and reconciled to God.

Other giants of the faith also left legacies of trust in God. Joshua's final charge to the people he led into the Promised Land was, "Choose for yourselves this day whom you will serve . . . But as for me and my household, we will serve the Lord" (Joshua 24:15). These words were consistent with how he'd lived his life, but restating them in the context of his nearing death was something he deemed necessary.

Who could forget the parting words of the apostle Paul to his spiritual son Timothy? "I have fought the good fight, I have finished the race, I have kept the faith. Now there is in store for me the crown of righteousness, which the Lord, the righteous Judge, will award to me on that day—and not only to me, but also to all who have longed for his appearing" (2 Timothy 4:7–8).

So, while the apple-a-day prescription for physically healthy aging may be to eat right, move right, and think right—the spiritual prescription is to fight the good fight of faith, and with God's provision maintain spiritual fruitfulness to one's last breath.

Closing **Prayer**

Father, God, I don't feel equipped to help my parent maintain a physically and spiritually healthy outlook. So I ask for Your wisdom in how to come alongside my parent and challenge him to do all that is necessary to maintain the best possible physical health. More importantly, I ask Your Spirit to challenge him to be spiritually fruitful in Your sight with every moment of life You give him. Amen.

Take *Action*

1. Talk with your parent about what spiritual legacy she wants to leave for your family.

2. Visit the National Institute on Aging's website at http://www.nih.gov/nia for suggestions on healthy aging, balanced diets for seniors, and healthy exercises.

3. Check with a church or local ministry to find volunteer projects your family can take on together with your parent — or if there are projects a parent can join himself.

4. Make a concerted effort to spend quality time in contact with your parent this week.

Chapter Four

VISITING
Nurse Kratchet

Tips and helps for

making the most of rehab

Marie's Father Regains His Breath

My dad has congestive heart failure. He had two bypasses and has had two stents put in. He had four bouts of pneumonia this year. He was in and out of the hospital from February until June—every ten days to two weeks found him back in ICU. Because of the pneumonia, he was dependent on oxygen. He was so weak and had lost so much weight—coming directly from the hospital back home would never have worked. He was limited in his walking without aid, so his internist suggested therapy. Early in the discussion, I realized this was not something that could be done outpatient—it would require checking him into a rehab center.

It took Dad awhile to catch on to this. When he found out he was going to live in a rehab center, it broke him.

The doctor gave us a list of four rehab centers she visits every week. This was a great benefit. I'd never heard of an internist visiting a rehab center and checking on her patients. But she did it, every week.

My brother and I took a day off work and visited every one of the centers on her list, looking for a place where Dad would be comfortable. Some were faith based, others weren't. We ended up with a faith-based facility. At each facility, we would be met by a patient coordinator who would walk us around. We'd see the rehab room where they'd work on his muscles, balance, and strength. We'd see the dining room and meet the staff.

We chose one that had just refurbished its rehab section—so everything was new. It was close to our homes, and it was one of those places that felt right when you walk in. It had bright, cheery rooms and a great fitness room for rehab. He'd have a private room with a private shower. When we talked with the staff at the nurse's station, we felt their goal for Dad and ours was the same.

We put a positive spin on it for Dad by telling him, "It's a big step up from hospital to rehab. The next step is from rehab to home. You're moving in the right direction."

It turned out to be a positive experience for Dad, even though he had to return three times—because of so many hospitalizations. He met and became friends with men his age. One had had a stroke; others were amputees awaiting prostheses. By comparison, Dad made amazing progress. He went there dependent on oxygen—and was weaned off of it. We consider it divine intervention that he is now breathing on his own.

AS I WAS THINKING about Marie's experience, we were eating lunch at our favorite family restaurant. There we saw some regulars we'd been missing lately. We'd seen the husband in the restaurant alone for several weeks while his wife was in rehab after knee replacement surgery. But today, they were back in together. She was looking thinner and a little tired (she'd just been worked over by her physical therapist)—but was wearing a bright smile.

We commented on how good it was to see her without a cane or walker. She grinned and replied, "I've had two knees replaced now, and all I can say is I'm glad God didn't give me three legs!" But she did concede that after the pain subsides—the sooner, the better—it will have been worth it.

She was walking better now than we'd seen her walk in years— even after a therapy session where she said, "I thought the girl was going to break my leg right off." When she said this, I thought of comedian Mark Lowry's "Pivot on Your Good Foot" routine, where a therapist kept telling Mark to walk toward her, pivoting on his good foot. He would reply, "Ma'am, I don't have a good foot. If you have one I can borr-ee, I'll be glad to pivot." It turned out, Mark's supposed "good foot" was broken in a way that didn't show up on X-rays. The routine always has audiences in stitches, and plays on stereotypes of rehab as lower on the fun continuum than a mouthful of root canals.

But what our restaurant friend reminded me is that, kidding aside, making good use of a professionally administered rehabilitation regimen can provide the best opportunity for our parents to regain maximum function after an injury or surgery.

Ask about Options

In the last three months, this friend experienced both of the two major classes of rehab: inpatient and outpatient.

Outpatient rehab may require a close partnership with a patient's family care team. When my dad was out of the hospital after bypass surgery, a rehab nurse came to visit him three times a week. She would walk him in circles around the first floor of our house—cajoling him into going farther each time she visited. She'd ask us to see that he kept up the same pace and frequency on days she didn't visit. She pushed him to do his exercises (Mom and I would stand at the kitchen island doing them ourselves, just to get him to cooperate); then she'd check his vital signs to be sure he wasn't doing too much, too soon.

Patients further along in recovery may benefit from rehab centers equipped with exercise equipment that rivals any premium gym.

These, too, are staffed with therapists to monitor and challenge patients to achieve recuperative goals. Our hospital offered this service to my dad, but he wasn't ready. Other friends who'd had similar surgeries to his benefited from visits to this specialized gym, and continued as long and as often as they were allowed.

But, in a day of insurance-dictated maximum hospital stays for every medical procedure, it may not be safe to discharge patients directly home after surgery. Instead, they may need to be monitored temporarily by medical professionals twenty-four hours a day. Here, especially, there are many decisions for a family to make carefully—and prayerfully.

Pam, whose ninety-four-year-old mother required a stay in rehab following a broken hip, says she and her brother based their decision on which facility to use by taking the advice of the hospital social worker, who gave them their family doctor's preferred facility—which happened to be "approximately between our two homes." Location does seem to be a big determining factor, as it was for Marie and her siblings.

But another deciding point gets to the nature of therapy. Many hospitals are creating inpatient rehab wards on their main campuses. Nurse Jeanette Giambolvo says this can offer big benefits: "In a hospital there are code blue teams present all the time, and there tends to be a higher level of staffing skill. There are always professional people there. Some free-standing rehab centers are good, but how is the public to know? One thing hospitals are having to do now is be rated according to how they perform. We have to post our ratings; they are publicized."

But not everyone is accepted to hospital rehab, even where it is available. Pam's mother didn't meet the hospital program's benchmarks three days after her surgery, so she had to be discharged to another facility. Initially, Pam and her brother were disappointed. But looking back, they are glad. "Had she remained in the hospital, she would have been wheeled out for therapy and returned to the room,"

Pam says. "But in the rehab center we chose, they put our mom out in the hall often to be around other people."

A Family that Participates

Pam says one of the reasons she felt her mother's rehab was a success was because, as she said, "The staff was available to us in person and by phone. The admissions nurse talked with us about Mom. More important, she listened to us. She also—and this is key—told us the name of the administrator we should contact in case there were any problems. We were welcome to visit any time. My brother and I both live close enough that we were able to go every day. After a few days, the staff knew us."

One common factor in nearly every success story is the family's active involvement. Hospital and rehab nurses gave Marie counsel she is anxious to pass along: "The nurses said, 'We know you kids are here. We see your faces. We know you love your father. That makes it easier for us to want to care for him and get him well.'" She believes her frequent presence, and that of her siblings, played a major role in the high-quality care her father received. "If you are a visible family member, the doctors and nurses will notice that and you will be surprised the attention the family member will get—because you are watching and involved with the patient."

Scoping Out the Territory

That participation begins before checking a parent in. As Marie and her brother did, in-person visits by family members can tell a great deal about the character of a place. They had fairly accurate first impressions of the places they visited—and they knew their dad's preferences and idiosyncrasies better than anyone.

In contrast, when my dad was coming out of the cardiac unit, the surgeon convinced him to sign himself into a facility. The hospital social worker gave Dad two options, and since he was familiar with one of them (two friends had been there), he chose it without giving us the opportunity to check out the place. In retrospect, he admits that was a bad choice.

What we didn't know was the facility had been sold to a conglomerate and was in transition. The head nurse was unavailable—Mom and I never did meet her. The nursing staff was composed of temporary employees who were there for just one shift. Worse yet, dementia patients and rehab patients were placed in one ward and our doctors would not be allowed to visit Dad there. Once he checked himself in, it was difficult to get him out.

To avoid experiences like ours, experts recommend looking for telltale signs. Chaplain Dale Sawyer, who holds weekly services and makes regular visits to a number of facilities, suggests asking:

* Is it environmentally attractive to the person who might be put in there? Is it a bright place, or dismal and dark?
* Is there clear one-on-one contact between the staff and the patients you see?
* Is it clean?
* Does it smell good?
* Did you note the arrangement of rooms?
* Are there four people stuffed into a room meant for two?

He says the mental, emotional, and spiritual setting has a great deal to do with the patient's physical progress. As a rule, the chaplain prefers Christ-oriented facilities over those owned and run by for-profit corporations. He says those who serve in the name of Christ seem to "provide loving care—yes, they take care of the medical things, but they do it in a loving way."

In choosing a facility for our parents—whether temporary or permanent (for more on nursing home choice, see chapter 11)—a good first impression is huge. Pam says of her first impression, "The lobby looked like a hotel, and the halls were well lighted and clean."

A Change of Mind

Checking a parent into rehab can make you feel as though you're abandoning her. That's another reason family participation is pivotal—to keep the parent engaged in family life and the adult child a key player in her parent's recovery.

Remember how Marie had to "sell" the rehab experience to her dad? Pam had to overcome her own stereotypes. "One thing I dreaded was knowing other people who were also elderly, hurt, sad, or ill would be there. I thought it would be depressing. Instead, I looked at other people as I wanted them to see our mom: as accomplished, intelligent, capable people who'd just gotten old. Not as people who'd always been at this stage of life and hadn't done anything else." This is an others-centered perspective that allowed Pam to be a positive influence on her mother at a frightening time.

Pam's positive attitude was reflected in (and reflective of) the attitudes of the professionals who cared for her mom (the facility was owned by a for-profit corporation). "The staff did not give up on her. The goal of the physical therapy program was to get her up and mobile enough to return to her home, where we had arranged through an agency for twenty-four-hour live-in care. It would have been easy to assume a ninety-four-year-old woman would never regain significant mobility."

In the final analysis, stays in a rehab center—or regular visits from Nurse Kratchet in one's home—aren't going to be comfy retreats in five-star hotels. They are going to require parents to put in hours of hard work to regain as much function as possible given their age and physical challenges. And they're going to require patience—from all involved.

I've never been much on patience. When I was a teen, a Bible study leader advised me, "Never pray for patience; God will just give you trials." And I never have! But, as you've surely found, we get this *gift* whether we pray for it or not. As the Bible says, "Count it all joy when you fall into various trials, knowing that the testing of your faith produces patience" (James 1:2–3 NKJV). The challenge to count rehab "as joy" brings to mind the biblical call to "run with endurance the race that is set before us, looking unto Jesus, the author and finisher of our faith, who for the joy that was set before Him endured the cross, despising the shame, and has sat down at the right hand of the throne of God" (Hebrews 12:1–2 NKJV).

Patient endurance may be the best our parents and we can muster during rehab—despite the cheeriest rooms and most compassionate staffs. And Christ's example—looking ahead at the end result (in His case, the salvation of our souls; in our parents' cases, regained strength and independence) can help us all keep putting in our best efforts for the duration.

Closing **Prayer**

God, I hate the idea of placing my parent in rehab. I'm frightened, and so is she. Please guide us—give us Your clear direction and wisdom as we visit facilities. Most of all, as we choose a rehab location, give us a patient, competent, caring staff to make it time well spent for my parent's recovery.

Take *Action*

1. If your parent is expecting to be hospitalized for a planned surgical procedure that requires rehab (like hip or knee replacement), visit facilities together before the surgery.

2. Ask for referrals from medical professionals and social workers. Check out www.MyZiva.net to find suggestions on how to choose an inpatient facility. Trust your gut instincts as you visit facilities or meet therapists.

3. Be ready to partner with the rehab team to help your parent get the most out of the therapy.

4. Be encouraging, motivating, and positive as you help your parent adjust to rehab.

Chapter Five

GRUMPY OLD MEN
(and Women)

Coping when loved ones direct

complaints at their caregivers

Laura's Housecleaning Adventure

I took yesterday off work because my husband and I needed to clean his mom's house. Fortunately I used comp time from a conference I attended recently and didn't have to spend a vacation day. His mom isn't physically (or, really, mentally) able to clean, and she fired the one cleaning service she had. Possibly because of her dementia, she's letting herself and everything else go.

My brother-in-law is coming in from California next week to both celebrate his mom's birthday and help my husband investigate assisted-living options, so we decided to go up there and just go at it.

I actually like to clean, but what a test of patience! She complained in that horrible, querulous way old people have. She complained about her poor son taking too long in the supermarket shopping for her *company*, she complained about him spending too much money (though she has more than enough), she complained that she wanted us to leave, she complained *about him having the temerity to change the sheets . . .*

Finally I lost it. I had vacuumed the two-story house from top to bottom, folded laundry, fixed lunch, dusted, polished silver, and cleaned two bathrooms, and my husband had been working equally hard. I just snapped, "How about saying, 'Thank you, it looks nice'?"

I still don't think she understood what I was getting at. She's always been kind of hard to deal with, and they say old age magnifies people's negative traits. Yes, I know dementia makes people combative. I'm glad we were able to help—but the elderly can be infuriating.

WHEN THE FILM *Grumpy Old Men* debuted in 1994, the premise was funny. Two elderly neighbor men putting on their best stereotypical crotchety 'tudes, sniping at each other and at others around them. It was so funny, in fact, that a sequel soon followed—*Grumpier Old Men*. More guffaws. Leave it to Walter Matthau and Jack Lemmon.

Bob Hope's former staff writer Martha Bolton would say this humorous take is healthy: "I'm convinced some things happen to us for the sheer comedy of it all—you know, so life doesn't get boring. Like any good drama, life has to have a bit of comic relief to ease the tension and rejuvenate our spirits."

In a fictional world these behaviors that my friend and fellow caregiver Laura would classify as *querulous* ("given to complaining; peevish"—I looked it up) can provide a brief repose and tension relief from real-world troubles. But live it with your parent in real time, and the humor turns sour faster than a gallon of milk in August's midday sun.

There may be good reason for the grumpy stereotype, though. Like most generalizations, it is rooted in some fact. When you think about one of its contributors, you'll realize it's not a surprising result.

Consider that in today's Western culture we attach few positive attributes to aging. Unlike the Eastern cultures, we don't innately respect aged experience. In fact, we eschew outward evidences of aging, stave it off like the plague, hide it at all costs. The antiaging industries of Botox and cosmetic surgeries and wrinkle creams and hair dyes and age-spot removers and spa treatments and exercise equipment are booming. Advertisers unabashedly court the young market. Their message? *Look young. Think young. Be young. Then you will be most valuable to society.*

If we allow culture to devalue our elders, how can we expect our parents to feel anything other than querulous when there is nothing more they can do to deny aging's merciless process of decelerating their bodies and minds?

How Much of the Stereotype Is True?

According to psychologist Alice Domar, the aging process can initiate several emotional responses in care receiver and caregiver. She says whatever coping mechanisms we've created through life as we've dealt with change will be magnified when we're confronted with age-associated change:

> They have lost the [people] they once were. They are likely to be grieving the loss of their ability to do the things they used to do. This grief manifests itself in many different ways. Symptoms of grief range from shock and disbelief, to denial that change is taking place, to depression, loneliness, and a sense of isolation. More visible emotions, such as panic, hostility, and an inability to function day-to-day, are also possible. Stubbornness, regression, and even rage can result from a sense of losing one's former self.[6]

Nurse Meghan says she noticed these emotions in her mother-in-law. She lists "fear, lack of trust, less ability to assimilate info, and less faith in God's ability to take care of her." But Meghan makes an observation: As her mother-in-law exhibited these traits, Meghan and her husband experienced the "developing emotional responses" of "impatience and frustration. Where was her faith? Why didn't she trust us?"

Perhaps you, as I, can relate. As the care receiver becomes agitated, we caregivers naturally respond by fighting back—escalating the issue. It's what Laura experienced in the story that opened this chapter. Even the most patient caregiver is tested to the limit when bombarded by wave after wave of incoming verbal—or physical—blasts. Eventually, the pressure needs to be vented to stave off a full-scale explosion.

Understanding that grief over lost independence may be at least partially to blame for a loved one's tirade may help temporarily, but we'll need more effective coping mechanisms if we're to find long-term pressure valves.

Easing the Tension

In 2002 the National Institutes of Health held a "Successful Aging" seminar. In synthesizing the information presented at the seminar Dr. Judy Salerno, who directs the NIH's National Institute on Aging, concluded, "Disease and disability are not inevitable consequences of aging." In other words, simply seeing signs of aging doesn't have to lead down a slippery slope of hopelessness or despair.

In support of Salerno's synthesis, University of Wisconsin professor Gloria Sarto told the conference that attitudes like self-esteem, quality relationships, defining life as meaningful and exercising some independence can help people age well. "Find something positive in the face of adversity," she said.[7]

If these findings are true, we caregivers can contribute toward more positive attitudes in our parents.

Helping Them Feel Loved

One of the first ways we can do this is by helping them feel loved. Since our personal methods of expressing and receiving love may differ from those of our parents, psychologist Gary Chapman's book *The*

Five Love Languages is helpful to study. Chapman's premise is that individuals use different ways, different languages, to express and receive love. It may be through words that I feel most loved. It may be through quality time, acts of service, giving of gifts, or tender touch.

For example, if words are my mother's primary love language, then spoken affirmation will lift her spirits. But if her love language is quality time, and I stuff her needs into scraps of time in my schedule—then even if I meet all her physical needs and say nice things to her when I'm with her, she'll feel unloved and she'll be more likely to lash out in anger. Feeling she wasn't receiving enough focused attention, one woman I know took a swing of her cane at her caregivers. Her basic needs were being met, but she wasn't "feeling the love."

Helping Them Feel Trustworthy

Experts agree another way to help our parents through the stages of aging is by affording them as much decision-making participation as possible. With advanced dementia patients, this won't be as feasible. But in general, the more we respond to their needs as team players rather than bosses, the calmer responses we'll receive from them. It's a matter of helping them feel that their physical limitations have not robbed them of the credibility they've worked a lifetime to establish.

In an article titled "Talking Points," Dr. Carol Anderson writes,

> When talking with your aging parents, it's important to use an approach that lets Mom or Dad know that you want to understand him or her better and that you are not trying to take over his or her life. Your approach should show a willingness to work together. . . . It's also important to emphasize Mom's or Dad's strengths rather than dwell on any weaknesses.[8]

Helping Them Feel Valuable

That last bit of counsel leads to another way we can have a positive impact on our parents' moods—by dwelling on their best assets. It's a biblical concept. Paul writes, "Fix your thoughts on what is true, and honorable, and right, and pure, and lovely, and admirable. Think about things that are excellent and worthy of praise" (Philippians 4:8b NLT). I resonate with that. I've often responded better to circumstances beyond my control when someone couched his comments with an acknowledgment of what I'd done right—rather than diving into a litany of my shortcomings.

Often it's our words that emphasize our parents' strengths, but sometimes words seem empty without harmonious action. Think back to Ruth and Naomi. Remember how bitter Naomi was in chapter 1? She said things like "My life is much too sad for you to share, because the Lord has been against me!" (v. 13 NCV). What comforted her at that moment was Ruth's persistent presence, along with her faith-filled words: "Don't ask me to leave you and turn back. Wherever you go, I will go; wherever you live, I will live" (v. 16 NLT).

Changing Ourselves
(If Not Our Loved Ones)

Okay. So that's the best-case scenario. But what if old age has magnified a parent's already-sour disposition, exacerbating a lifelong painful relationship? What if no positive talk or loving action can help? That's when another savvy life principle kicks in: even if we can't change someone else's behavior, we can still change our own.

Curbing Our Own Querulous-ity

When I was in high school preparing to travel with a summer singing group, we were required to memorize a long list of Scriptures.

Most were for others' benefit: teaching us to lead others in a salvation prayer, to pray for others' needs, to encourage people toward godliness. But one verse was especially for us—to make the summer pass uneventfully (if you don't count trailer tire blowouts or the van overheating). The verse? Philippians 2:14: "Do everything without complaining and arguing" (NLT). Funny, that has stayed with me for twenty-five years. Not that I've always practiced it. But I've always been convinced of its wisdom. It's parallel to another Pauline admonition: "If possible, on your part, live at peace with everyone" (Romans 12:18 HCSB).

As we're going about changing our attitudes toward cantankerous care receivers, consciously laying down our rights to dispute with them may be one immediate answer. That much depends on us. I remember a psychologist describing this choice to me years ago. He said that in every crisis we have three options: put up our dukes and fight, run the other way and flee, or lie back and ride out the wave.

Later, when we discuss becoming our parents' advocate in medical situations, we'll look into the put-up-your-dukes option—because fighting *for* their best interests may be lifesaving. But fighting *against* our parents is counterproductive.

Fleeing, at least as a long-term solution, probably isn't an option. (Although short-term flight respites are necessary.) So consciously choosing to go with the flow may be the most feasible choice.

Don't you feel a chink of the chain binding you fall away? Options and choices return control to us—and that's a good thing.

Turning to Prayer and Friendship

Whether or not we're dealing with a difficult parent, we'll need praying friends to help hold us accountable and offer a semblance of sanity. Jill Briscoe writes in *Thank You for Being a Friend*, "We can reach out and take the hand of whoever is nearest to us and stand against [Satan] in the name of Jesus, our Captain and Savior. We can pray! Whenever we do we will experience and know a closeness with those we pray with that we didn't know before—it's called 'prayer friendship.'"

And, if you're dealing with the best-case scenario of a believing parent who doesn't mean to be querulous, Jill says, "Prayer is a place where even relatives, like a mother and daughter, can become closer friends."

Another Look at the Humor

We may yet have one more choice in our arsenals. Martha Bolton writes in her book *When the Going Gets Tough, The Tough Start Laughing,* "With everything that may come our way, we can still have joy. Not a joy that denies or discounts pain, but a joy that wells up inside of us *in spite of it.*"

Years ago, when I was managing editor of *The Standard,* I saw this modeled by an interview I did for a cover story in our magazine. Dorothy was a widow succumbing to Alzheimer's disease. Her daughter Roberta, the mom of teenagers, couldn't dedicate full-time to her mother's care. So God led her to Mary, who was working her way through college to prepare for career missions. Mary needed a home; Dorothy needed a companion. The situation was ideal.

I interviewed Mary, and she told this story that, while sad, became a source of lighthearted banter for Roberta and the caregiving team:

There were times when Dorothy would break out into the song, "Chatta, chatta, chatta, chatta, ching, ching, ching," and dance the Charleston. She must not have remembered that she was pushing ninety, because she would kick so high she'd almost knock herself over!

I would come home to all of the meat from the freezer defrosting for dinner, or the laundry room would be flooded because she would hear the sound of the washing machine and think it was broken, so she would pull all of the wash out during the rinse cycle.

And of course, there were the numerous occasions when Dorothy would move all the patio furniture into the house, because, she reasoned, furniture didn't belong outside.

In all these situations, Mary had a choice—and, young woman of wisdom that she was—she chose to lay back, go with the flow, and have a good belly laugh.

Closing **Prayer**

God, some days I don't see the humor in my situation. I wish life would roll back to a time before old age began encroaching on our family. I need You to equip me with the words and deeds to build up my parent and encourage her to feel loved and valued. Help me respond in love, rather than anger—no matter what frustration she tosses my way.

Take *Action*

1. Read Gary Chapman's *The Five Love Languages* to find clues on how each member of your household, including your care receiver, will feel most loved.

2. Make an effort to help your parent participate in his own care.

3. Try to identify the humor in a situation that is escalating to tirade status.

4. Enlist trusted friends as prayer partners to support you.

Chapter Six

WHERE EVERYBODY
Knows Your Name

Preparing for chronic

doctor's office visits

Julie's Mom—A Reluctant Patient

I knew Mom had cataracts but didn't know much about the condition. I'd shuttle her to the optometrist every few weeks, where her prescription kept changing. Her dressing table sported a selection of different-strength contact lenses that rivaled a small warehouse—and still she carried four pairs of glasses—one for organ, one for piano, one for choir music (when she wore those, she couldn't see the director), and one for driving. Even then, I surreptitiously followed behind, cleaning up toaster crumbs and pesky spills she couldn't see—and wouldn't ever ask her to read a street sign.

The optometrist kept recommending an ophthalmologist. But, since she was going into the exams alone while I waited outside, Mom didn't let on that it was urgent. She'd heard horror stories of cataract surgery gone awry, so she wanted no part of it. "I'll live with it," she'd tell me.

One Sunday I was waiting to exit the sanctuary, and I overheard our *friend Jeanette telling another woman that she and her husband had just had cataracts removed from all four of their eyes. Rudely, I interjected myself into their conversation. Yes, I'd heard right—a four-for-four record. Jeanette's eyes sparkled. Two days later, I received an envelope from Jeanette containing a brochure on the procedure and the doctor's number. I had Mom call Jeanette and hear for herself what a good experience it had been.*

Not quite kicking and screaming, Mom agreed to an appointment. This time I went into the exam, and to my consternation she couldn't discern the difference between the E and the W on the eye chart's top line. But the doctor was encouraging, saying she was a prime candidate for cataract surgery. He scheduled the procedures, one eye at a time.

In recovery after the first surgery, Mom could see perfectly out of her "new eye." In comparing the two, she realized how dreadful her sight had become. When we talked to the surgeon after the second surgery, Dad asked him to put Mom's cataracts back in—because she was seeing too much (translation, Dad was now getting in trouble for the messes he leaves in his wake). Actually, she was seeing 20/20.

Every time Mom returns to the surgeon's office for follow-up, he chuckles over Dad's impertinence and grins proudly over the quality of life he was able to return to her because she finally agreed to come to him.

I AM NOT A MEDICAL professional (far from it; I deftly substituted computer science and nutrition classes for chemistry, biology, and physics to fulfill my collegiate science requirements). But this chapter, more than any others, I've lived.

In the past three weeks with my two parents, I've logged ten trips to doctors' offices at two hospitals—including two surgeries, three ultrasounds, two EKGs, more blood draws than any vampire could ever dream of using, six pacemaker readouts, two chest X-rays, six specialists, dozens of health questions . . . and a partridge in a pear tree. Well, maybe not the partridge, but you'll find everything else in my Outlook logs. The receptionist in Dad's cardiologist's office is threatening to charge me rent on the waiting room chair, and we're on a first-name basis with the techs in the hospital's cardiac cath lab—even if I don't quite know what a cardiac *cath* is.

We've dealt with sweet, understanding medical staffs in some offices and gruff, careless workers in others. At times, I've had to fight to get past gatekeepers to assure my parents of the treatments they need, while other times I've stood by as others treat my parents with the tender care they'd expect their parents to receive.

Making Time

Even with relatively healthy parents, medical office visits for routine exams and refilling prescriptions are a regular way of life for most adult children.

The other day I was in a store I frequent often, a mom-and-pop operation where I've come to know the proprietor fairly well. As I told her I was writing this book, she poured out her heart. She runs shuttle service for her seventy-year-old mom, making at least three doctor's appointments each week. That in addition to regular hours at work and being available for her teenaged daughter and her husband/business partner. She's overwhelmed to the point of tears.

For every one of us who feels equally overwhelmed by responsibilities for work, household, and parents' chronic medical conditions, her plight rings true. How do we do it all? It's not a question of, when is it time for me? Rather, it's a question of, how can I find enough hours to please everyone?

Here's a newsflash—you can't. So stop trying.

Whew! Did I really mean that? Yep. If you're responsible for your parent's care, along with everything else in your life, something has to give.

For some caregivers, the something that gives is career. They choose to take family leave (the Family and Medical Leave Act requires employers of more than fifty people to offer you twelve weeks of unpaid leave to care for a family member). Dean, whom we'll meet again in chapter 10, moved across country to care for his ailing mother and built a home where she could move around comfortably. He has used all his allotted family leave time and every hour of vacation time in caring for his mother. Other career sacrifices may mean scaling back to "the mommy track"—taking less-demanding work at lesser pay, or choosing to tighten your spending so you can go part-time.

If we can't scale back at work, we can still streamline our schedules. It may mean resigning from church or community or school committees. It may mean missing sporting events for your kids (not an unpardonable sin). It may mean getting help from spouse, siblings, children, or outside services for household chores and meal preparation.

All I can tell you is: something has to give. Here's the reality: Doctors and specialists work on their own timetables. We are subject to their schedules. We may be left waiting for hours just to eke out a few brief moments of their time.

One trick I've found helpful is to schedule the earliest appointment, first thing in the morning. That means we catch the doctor when he's fresh, unharried, and not as backed up by delays as at the end of the day.

My other trick is to bring work with me—at least for my time in the waiting room. I pack files and a laptop computer and can work just about anywhere for an hour or two. This helps keep my attitude positive, because I don't feel my time is being wasted, and helps control my harriedness by keeping at least one project on schedule. My parents understand this and help me guard quiet time while I'm waiting with them.

Daughter and caregiver Marie is a flight attendant whose schedule tends to be more flexible than her three siblings'. Even so, sometimes an appointment conflicts with her travel/work plans. At first, she would fret and call her employer. But now, she's become a little more assertive: "If I have to work, I will call to reschedule at the doctor's office. They can usually get me an appointment for Dad within a day or two around the original plan—and I can be there without missing [or jeopardizing] more work."

Physicians and the Great Physician

But time elements aside, the greatest concern we have is helping our parents assemble the best medical teams for their special needs. Probably my favorite gospel writer is Luke—the physician. His well-researched and documented reporting of Jesus' interactions with ailing people engages my emotions and rings true to life. So when he tells the story of a paralyzed man whose friends carry him to Jesus—even cut out a hole in a home's roof to lower him in front of Jesus (Luke 5:17–26), I stop and listen. What strikes me about Luke's telling of this story is the friends' tenacity. They won't stop at anything to get their patient the care he needs. There must be consequences for tearing off someone's roof—not to mention muscle strain from lowering the man through the hole. Yet we don't see self-concern—only concern that the man get an audience with the Great Physician.

This motivates us to make the same effort for our parents—to get them to the best medical professional we can find. It means not allowing ourselves to be stopped by the roadblock of waiting twelve weeks for the first available appointment. I can't tell you how many times I've had success asking to be called in case anyone cancels before our appointment date.

It also means not allowing our parents to settle for a physician who dismisses their symptoms as part of "growing old." Recently I sat in a caregiving seminar led by home care physician Dr. Thomas Cornwell, who says it's usually a cop-out when a doctor blames a condition on old age. He advised that we search for doctors intent on locating the core cause of an ailment.

Perhaps the biggest element of choosing the best physician is that it be someone in whom our parents and we have confidence. We don't have to be buddies—often the best-qualified specialists have all the bedside manner of Attila the Hun. But what we need is healthy respect and understanding. We need to be confident in the doctor's expertise and convinced he has paid enough attention to our parents' symptoms and test results to create the best care plan.

When my dad began experiencing heart symptoms and we suspected he would require bypass surgery, we did research about cardiac hospitals. We learned our closest hospital had experienced a 100 percent turnover in cardiac unit staffing. This made us uneasy. So we found a hospital a few miles away whose cardiac unit ranked among the top 100 in the country. We got a referral to a cardiologist there. When we met him, we knew immediately he was a good fit—because he smiled and listened with compassion and treated Dad like a real person. That referral led to Dad's successful six-bypass surgery. We still see that cardiologist regularly.

According to the National Institute of Health's Senior Health website our experience was typical—and well advised: "How well you and your doctor talk to each other is one of the most important parts of getting good health care. In the past, the doctor typically took the lead and the patient followed. Today, a good patient-doctor relationship is a partnership."[9]

Keeping Accurate Records

Whether we're seeking medical care for our parents' chronic or life-threatening conditions, we'll need to be prepared for each appointment. We need to have with us complete medical histories—including dates and details on surgeries and medical tests, immunization records, contact information for other doctors who treat them, medication allergies, symptoms of current ailments, lists and dosages of medications (over-the-counter, prescription, supplements, and vitamins), insurance and Medicare information.

If gathering that information sounds overwhelming, there are a number of medical organizers on the market to help assemble it. One of the least expensive, yet comprehensive, organizers is the Personal Health Care Passport (see appendix 2 for contact information). Its creator, Melissa Kahn, says it's important that such an organizer "promotes coordinated care" and "empowers people during a time when they might feel powerless in making difficult decisions." Her product is small enough to keep in a pocket or purse.

Another option is the binder-based So Tell Me Personal Health Organizer.

I keep this information in my PDA, which seldom leaves my side and synchronizes regularly with my desktop computer—so it's available whenever I need it.

Asking the Right Questions

Another element of preparation is to help our parents prepare a list of topics to discuss with the doctor. It may be questions about a diagnosis, concerns about a test or surgical procedure, or observations about new symptoms. Usually we'll have time for three or four topics during one consultation, so prioritizing this list is crucial. According to the NIH,[10]

Making a list of your symptoms before your visit will help you not forget to tell the doctor anything. Symptoms can be physical, such as pain, fever, a lump or bump, unexplained weight gain or loss, change in energy level, or having a hard time sleeping. Your list should include:

  ✳ what the symptom is
  ✳ when it started
  ✳ what time of day it happens and how long it lasts
  ✳ how often it happens

* anything that makes it worse or better
* anything it prevents you from doing.

Then, when we're in the office with our parent, one good use of our time is to take notes. We can ask if there are DVDs or brochures that explain a condition, procedure, or new medication. If there aren't any in the office, we can find a plethora of information by searching the Internet. This morning I signed on to www.ask.com to find out about a medication recently prescribed for Dad. It would take only moments for you to do the same.

For the Waiting Room Sitter

In the *He Cares New Testament,* the devotional beside Matthew 25:31–40 contains a word of encouragement for those who carve time out of hectic schedules to shuttle parents to medical appointments.

Here Jesus tells the story of His sheep who stand before Him ready to receive their reward. He invites them, "Come, you who are blessed by my Father; take your inheritance . . . [For] I was sick and you looked after me. . . . I tell you the truth, whatever you did for one of the least of these brothers of mine, you did for me" (vv. 34–36, 40,).

That's where the devotion picks up:

When you took off work to go to the doctor with your loved one, you did it for Jesus. . . . When you got up in the middle of the night to get more pain medicine, you did it for Jesus. When you rubbed a back, cooled a brow, cleaned up a mess, and sat through another long test, you did it for Jesus. Whether or not you got any appreciation from your loved one here and now, Jesus saw your kindness and He will bless you for it.

Closing **Prayer**

God, I take seriously the challenge of the paralytic's friends—to carry my parents first to You, the Great Physician, and then to qualified medical professionals. Help me be wise in helping my parents locate the best doctors, and give me the ability to take the time to be there with them whenever possible. Please equip me with all I need to fulfill Your purposes for my parents' medical care—whether or not I receive any accolades for it.

Take *Action*

1. Talk with your parent about how she feels about the health care she's receiving. Take seriously concerns she has. Whenever possible, ask your parent for permission to meet her doctors.

2. Visit the National Institute of Health's Senior Health website. Read the article and take the quiz about talking with your doctor (http://nihseniorhealth.gov/talkingwithyourdoctor/toc.html).

3. With your parent's help, prepare information to bring to his doctor's appointments. If you need help assembling this, find a medical history organizer (see appendix 2).

4. Visit websites that describe medications your parents take; or talk with a pharmacist about your parent's medications to be sure there aren't interactions between them.

Chapter Seven

SHOWDOWN
@ High Noon

Becoming the patient

advocate your parent needs

Olivia: Taking Responsibility for Mom's Medical Care

When Mom moved in with me, we had to get her new doctors. At each visit she would ask me to come in with her. I would sit quietly during each visit unless I was asked a question directly. The doctor would always talk to her.

Now we're into our third year, and she can't remember the answers anymore. For a while she would turn to me, and the doctor would ask me the questions—while trying to make her feel respected. I realized she was feeling embarrassed that she didn't remember. Now, I pretty much answer all the questions. But I am careful to say things like, "Isn't that right, Mom?"

I'm now established with all her medical team as her caregiver. They will talk to me about her care. They are cautious about violating a patient's rights and giving out information. It's good that I've established this pattern and relationship with her doctors during day-to-day appointments, because in crisis time, it was crucial.

This year, osteoporosis has become a major issue, causing fractures and two surgeries for Mom. We had decisions to make regarding placing Mom in an extended care facility after her most recent surgery. In that decision her primary care physician was especially helpful. I asked her what to do. She recommended a facility where she said she'd place her own mother were she in the same situation.

I ended up having a phone conversation with the doctor. The doctor was cautious in what she said to me, but essentially, she told me I had to make the decisions, doing the best I can for Mom. She recommended that when Mom is available, I ask her approval.

Essentially, though, this is uncharted territory. It is giving Mom the opportunity to trust my brothers and me. We said we would take care of her. And we have this opportunity to demonstrate love and respect in response to the trust she's placed in us.

THERE IS LITTLE MORE overwhelming in our caregiving journey than the moment we are thrust into making life-altering decisions about our parents' medical care. Usually these arise at crisis moments, when we are feeling distressed, fearful, saddened, or panicked. Yet, we can't afford to make the wrong choices—because life and death may hang in the balance.

That said, there are things we can do to put ourselves in the best position to speak up for our parents' best interests, like Olivia does with her mother's day-to-day and special-circumstance medical issues.

When They Can't Speak for Themselves

As I always do when faced with an overwhelming situation, I turned to the Scriptures to see if I could find a pattern for how to be God-honoring in our responsibilities to speak for our loved ones when they need it most. Not surprisingly, I found that Jesus wasn't silent about issues that arise for advocates.

One relevant story is the parable Jesus told about the "Good

Samaritan." Jesus holds up to us this man's example of caring for someone who couldn't speak up for himself—the man who was attacked by robbers and left for dead at the side of the road.

> "But a Samaritan, as he traveled, came where the man was; and when he saw him, he took pity on him. He went to him and bandaged his wounds, pouring on oil and wine. Then he put the man on his own donkey, took him to an inn and took care of him. The next day he took out two silver coins and gave them to the innkeeper. 'Look after him,' he said, 'and when I return, I will reimburse you for any extra expense you may have'" (Luke 10:33–35).

Here we have a model of a caregiver/advocate. First, the Samaritan felt compassion and did what he could to care for this sufferer. When it was obvious he needed assistance, he enlisted a professional—offering resources and incentive for the stranger's good care. In making sure the innkeeper knew he'd be returning to check on the man's care, the Samaritan was providing more than money—he was reminding the caregiver he'd answer to someone for the man's appropriate and tender treatment. Would the innkeeper have cared for the injured man without this incentive? We don't know, but the Samaritan felt it necessary to offer that reminder, just in case.

But that's not the only advocate example we'll find from Jesus. In fact, one of His roles is as our advocate before the Father. He is the mediator who puts Himself on the line for our best interests. Listen to the way the apostle John described Jesus' role: "We have an advocate who pleads our case before the Father. He is Jesus Christ, the one who is truly righteous. He himself is the sacrifice that atones for our sins—and not only our sins but the sins of all the world" (1 John 2:1–2 NLT). This is a role He fulfills with love, grace, and compassion—tirelessly, without regard to whether we deserve His sacrifice. (By the way, we don't deserve it—but He advocates for us in spite of ourselves.)

In these pictures of caring advocates, I find motivation and encouragement in taking responsibility for the care of my loved ones when they need it.

Surgeon and conference speaker Vicki Rackner, M.D., defines a patient advocate as "someone who promotes the best interests of the patient. A family caregiver can serve as an advocate and help a friend or relative take the fastest, most direct course from illness to optimal health. . . . It does not require specialized medical training."[11]

This advocate role puts us on the same team as the medical professionals treating our parents. I've had occasion to be tenacious (picture momma tiger protecting her cubs) about seeing that my dad get the surgeries he needs in a timely fashion. But even when fighting for a patient's rights, I remind myself that the doctors and I aren't meeting for a showdown at high noon behind the corral; we are fighting side by side with the same goal, the highest quality of care for the patient.

Permission to Advocate

But in this era of privacy rights, obtaining permission to advocate for our parents is crucial. Medical professionals are prohibited by law from releasing personal medical information to anyone without the care receiver's permission. (We'll get into the legal aspects of this in chapter 22.)

Dr. Rackner says the number one mistake caring people make is failing to obtain a patient's permission to act as his advocate:

> Be sure to get permission to step into the patient advocacy role. You could say, "I love you and want the best for you. Would you like me to help you get the quality of medical care I want you to have?" Don't second guess the answer. If the answer is no, clarify your role.[12]

There may be times, as in an emergency situation, when a patient is incapacitated and cannot make decisions for himself. But more often, at least in the early stages of watching our parents age, the permission comes from a perfectly competent parent who wants to have a second set of ears listen in on medical conversations and double-check instructions. Or she may want us to ask questions she's too intimidated or nervous to ask her doctor.

This happens in our house all the time. Seldom does any one of us (myself included) go into a doctor's exam room without one of the others present. Our family doctor knows to expect us two-by-two. The nurses in his office call Mom and me "the twins." I'm not quite sure how to take that, since she's significantly older than I; but I choose to think it's because she looks and acts so *young*.

Actually, my sixty-nine-year-old mom is vibrant and healthy. But when she had to visit a new thyroid specialist two months ago, she asked me to sit in on the appointment. Much like Olivia's experience in the opening story, we found the doctor amenable to having both of us present—but addressing most of his conversation to Mom. I was tempted to jump in with answers to his questions—but I restrained myself, offering only a brief prompt when it was called for; for example, when he asked her to list all the surgeries she's ever had, I reminded her of one she missed. It was good for her to have me there, because I was able to remind her of his directions and later restate for her the reasons for the tests he ordered.

Likewise, when it comes to treatment options, Mom and Dad know I'm available to offer opinions (I *always* have an opinion) when asked. But that's the key—*when asked*. Their medical decisions—like which kind of pacemaker or defibrillator Dad chooses to have implanted—are theirs to make. I'll get online and print out information they'd like to have. But they are competent to make the final choices themselves.

Shifting Roles during Hospitalization

The role does shift when a parent checks into the hospital. At check-in for my dad's recent hospitalizations, he was asked to designate at least one person to contact for emergency decisions. At the outset the hospital wants to know whom Dad designates as an advocate—with whom the medical team can share information and who will be making decisions while Dad is unable to do so himself.

As one of his advocates, I ask many questions—of Dad and of the medical staff. Of Dad, I make certain I know what he expects out of the procedure and gently ask what to do in case something doesn't go as expected. If it's difficult for you to do this with your parent, doctors suggest trying a role-playing exercise during a low-stress time. Nurse Jeanette says, "You have to be absolutely sure you know what that patient wants."

Of the hospital staff, I ask different questions. Say an orderly shows up in his room with an order to take him to a test—I'll ask which doctor ordered the test and make sure Dad's name is on the order. The same goes for medication.

Dad knows what his morning and afternoon pills look like. When the hospital provides a name-brand pill (rather than his usual generic) and it's a different shape and color, he recognizes it and calls one of us to make sure it's the same formula. That's our role.

Jeanette says, "It is immediately obvious to the medical professional who only sees you in time of crisis, if a family is truly involved with a loved one's care. The involved family *presents* with the patient immediately. There is a tender, loving relationship."

Advocating in Extenuating Circumstances

If you're not able to perform this advocate role for your loved one—because of physical distance or an emotionally charged history, for example—there is a category of professional caregivers called "geriatric care managers." It can be an expensive service, but a worthwhile role to have filled—as an aging parent, no matter how sharp in normal circumstances, may not be able to oversee his own inpatient care.

When Pastor Colin Smith preached through the Ten Commandments several years ago, he defined *honor* in a memorable way: "It means *to give weight to* your parents . . . to give weight to their needs and their interests. I have found no one formula as to how that should be done." Even with abusive parents or strained relationships, he says, "Properly understood, the commandment makes no difference. I want to speak sensitively to the person in this kind of situation. No one can prescribe what you must do." He elaborated by explaining that seeing to a parent's needs—by meeting them yourself or providing caring professionals to meet the needs you aren't able to meet—can all be part of fulfilling that commandment.

The ER Decision

Perhaps the largest challenge we face as nonprofessional patient advocates is that most of us aren't medically trained. Recognizing the time to step in may be difficult.

Mom and I ran into this issue on a day that started out ordinary. On our way out of the office, we stopped at Gram's apartment to check on her. We found her dehydrated—but refusing care. We sat with her for over an hour and pumped fluids into her. She perked up and said she wanted to sleep—that she'd be okay. She asked us to leave. We complied but returned after allowing her a reasonable nap time. She was now worse. Therefore, we overrode Gram's wishes and called an ambulance.

Later in the ER, we found ourselves wondering just when it's appropriate to call 911, even against a parent's wishes. In answer, I found this list of symptoms requiring an ER visit, prepared by the American College of Emergency Physicians. According to ACEP,[13] an emergency room visit is necessary for any of these symptoms:

* Difficulty breathing, shortness of breath
* Chest or upper abdominal pain or pressure
* Fainting, sudden dizziness, weakness
* Changes in vision
* Confusion or changes in mental status
* Any sudden or severe pain
* Uncontrolled bleeding
* Severe or persistent vomiting or diarrhea
* Coughing or vomiting blood
* Suicidal feelings
* Difficulty speaking
* Shortness of breath
* Unusual abdominal pain

This is a list I'm committing to memory, so if the situation arises again, I'll be armed to make a timely, informed advocacy decision.

Closing **Prayer**

God, here is another instance where I feel unqualified. I need Your supernatural wisdom and Your Holy Spirit's compassion to become the advocate for my parent. I don't know what's in his best interests, but You do. So, please direct my words and my actions—and put in our path a caring, compassionate medical team.

Take *Action*

1. Initiate a conversation (or role play) with your parent about whether she feels she needs help interpreting what her doctors are recommending.

2. If you're shuttling him to medical appointments, ask your parent's permission to sit in on the exam or consultation to listen silently.

3. If your parent is expecting to be hospitalized, find out whom he wants to make decisions while he is unable to do it for himself. Be sure that person is available and has an understanding of your parent's wishes.

4. If a family member isn't able to be your parent's advocate, consider hiring a geriatric care manager to oversee her medical program. A Web search for "geriatric care managers" should yield options near your parent's home.

Chapter Eight

DIVINE SECRETS
of the Dwindling
Sisterhood

Helping parents cope with

losing friends and family

Melissa's Mom Loses Her Circle

M*y mom was a pastor's wife—and a social maven. Her whole life re-volved around being first lady of the church my dad pastored. Every Friday for decades without fail, she and her club of church women would meet at a swanky downtown restaurant for lunch and shopping. They'd have prepared their husbands' dinners ahead, so they'd have the maximum "dishing" and browsing time. They were inseparable.*

Then one of the ladies contracted cancer and died. Soon after, another moved to the Sunbelt with her husband. Several husbands died, as did my father. It wasn't long before the group of "girls" wobbled on walkers, slouched in wheelchairs, rasped with oxygen tanks, and succumbed to infirmity. In the blink of an eye Mom—now homebound—was the only one left. To make things worse, Mom's big family of siblings dwindled to herself and one other. In retirement, she'd become close to her siblings and their spouses—taking vacations with them, having meals together several times a week, and socializing on all the major holidays. Suddenly, she found herself in her tenth decade, wondering why God would leave her here on earth when He'd already taken all of her contemporaries and most of her loved ones.

So one day she decided she wasn't going to eat anymore. She, whose first love was church and second love was eating (and who had lived to find ways to combine those two), had given up both. It lasted for nearly a week. We tried everything to entice her. Favorite foods. Undivided attention. Anything we could think of. Eventually hunger got the better of her, and a bowl of carryout soup started her back on solid food. But the experience scared us, because neither her faith nor our love seemed enough to sustain her through these dark days.

IN OUR TIME TOGETHER one word has been seldom spoken but always on the cusp of our concern: change. Now it is time for us to speak it and address it straight out.

This is a chapter about change—change from our parents' perspectives. You might guess from the wordplay in the chapter title that we'll be considering the upheaval of change in our parents' closest relationships: spouses, peers, colleagues, church families, business associates, friends. As our parents are aging, so are their contemporaries. "Duh," you may say. "That goes without saying." But does it? Perhaps you, like I, have failed to take into account the affect their shrinking social circles have on our parents' outlooks. People they have known for lifetimes are gone for good. Their worlds are becoming smaller, more limited, more isolated. It can be a not-happy time for them. Or not. It's up to them—and us.

I remember my dad's mom, who was widowed for more than twenty years. Even well into her eighties, Nannie would look around at other widow ladies in the church and say with a sigh and a choke in her voice, "She's a poor widow." But Nannie never considered that she was one, herself—she would have bristled at the thought.

Her attitude was that everyone else had sad, tragic lives, but hers wasn't so bad by comparison—she was doing just fine, thank-you-very-much. She had seen more than her share of change—in declining health and unable to get out to church, she'd had a broken shoulder, watched two sons-in-law die prematurely, and moved 1,500 miles from her longtime home. Yet she embraced these changes, made the most of her circumstances, and considered others more needy than herself.

Nannie may be more exception than rule, if aging expert Alice Domar's assessment is any indication. Dr. Domar writes,

> The emotions people experience as they cope with the changes that age brings on can be very similar to the emotions people feel when they lose a loved one. . . . This grief manifests itself in many different ways. Symptoms of grief range from shock and disbelief, to denial that change is taking place, to depression, loneliness, and a sense of isolation. More visible emotions, such as panic, hostility, and an inability to function day-to-day, are also possible. [14]

Few would argue that these turbulent emotions are the starting point as we face loss and change, but if we want to help our parents move into a *productive* new normalcy, a few "divine secrets" may provide the impetus we need.

Divine Secret 1: Embrace Grief

Here's a secret that frees us to experience the range of human emotions: Death made Jesus weep. Which Sunday school child hasn't padded her memory verse list with "Jesus wept"? (Okay, smarty, where's it found?) Let's examine the context of that little verse (it's John 11:35, by the way), because it has something important to offer our grieving parents.

It's planted in the middle of the story about the death of Jesus' friend Lazarus. Jesus' tears were genuine and striking to those who saw them. Given the context we can surmise they might have encompassed: sadness at the painful death Lazarus had endured, empathy with the sorrow of Mary and Martha, and anger at this brazen evidence of the fact that for a time His Father was allowing death to exist, as a consequence of sin.

The study note in the *Believer's Bible Commentary* reads, "He shed real tears of grief when He witnessed the terrible effects of sin on the human race. The fact that Jesus wept in the presence of death shows it is not improper for Christians to weep when their loved ones are taken. However, Christians do not sorrow as others who have no hope."

Maybe it's not a bad thing after all for Sunday school children to cut corners in learning this verse. What a powerful concept. Death makes God sad: its separation, its tragedy, its temporary finality.

Yes, *temporary* finality. Just as in this context Jesus knew what He was about to do—demonstrate His ultimate authority over death by raising Lazarus to life—we have insight into what Jesus is about to do for all with faith in Him. We too are about to be raised to life—unending life in paradise with Him. That's why Christians can experience the range of emotions—with the exception of hopelessness. We have hope that will not disappoint us, hope of a future He promised to His followers: "I am going there to prepare a place for you. And if I go and prepare a place for you, I will come back and take you to be with me that you also may be where I am" (John 14:2b–3).

Divine Secret 2: Allow for a Season of the Blues

Embracing grief without losing hope leads to the second "divine secret," letting our parents' grief be expressed and run its course. A season of sadness is healthy—much more so than stuffing emotions and pretending everything is A-OK.

As we saw, Melissa watched her mother go through a season of sadness, resulting from a string of losses that tore away at her support system and social network. Part of the elder woman's distress may have been an expression of survivor guilt. Many times, the daughter heard her mom say things like, "Why did God leave me here and take all my friends and loved ones? Why didn't I get to go to heaven when they did? Why did I have to stay here?" It can be a helpless feeling to hear a parent verbalize emotions like these. But know this: it's normal. We haven't looked in on the book of Ruth for a while, but now would be a good time to revisit that story. Survivor guilt is evident in Naomi's words upon returning home to Bethlehem, widowed and sorrowing. Her words sound remarkably like Melissa's mom's: "'Don't call me Naomi,' she told [her old friends]. 'Call me Mara [meaning bitterness], because the Almighty has made my life very bitter. I went away full, but the Lord has brought me back empty'" (Ruth 1:20).

Had I been Ruth, I probably would have elbowed Naomi and blurted, "What am I? Chopped liver? You're not empty! I guess I don't count for anything good, huh? Why did I ever bother coming with you?"

That's just me. But Ruth did something better—and wiser. She let Naomi vent. She gave her the benefit of being comforted by the women of the city. We have no evidence that she interrupted or contradicted Naomi. She may have even shed tears herself, for Naomi's loss and her own. Weeping with those who weep is a biblical concept (Romans 12:15) and a great lesson in helping our parents move through the emotions of their topsy-turvy, changing worlds.

Divine Secret 3: Not Everyone Responds the Same Way

While there are many similar responses and stages of grief, not everyone experiences every textbook stage; and even when people do experience the stages in typical progression, they move through each stage at different speeds—and need different levels of support. So we'll let this be "divine secret" number three.

Ava experienced this with her widowed mom. She and her sister Samantha felt it their responsibility to "bring Mom out" of her grief after their father died. She recalls, "We tried too hard to encourage Mom to go out, rather than just staring at the TV while we were away at work. We kept telling her to *do* something. But every time we tried, she wouldn't receive it well." The three even went to a church-sponsored grief support group, at the insistence of a friend. But the timing wasn't right—and the group wasn't a good fit. Ava recalls it ended up doing more harm than good. Eventually the sisters backed off, realizing their mom "had to go through the process in her own way, in her own time."

At the other end of the spectrum, Barbara took her widowed mom to a grief support group at their church. Both found the group significant in helping them process their sorrow. They benefited from the study that integrated Scripture. They found camaraderie among fellow believers who were going through the same emotions they were.

How can you tell if your parent is more like Ava's or Barbara's—ready to face her grief head-on and be drawn out or wanting the privilege of working through it quietly and alone? Trial and error, I suppose. And gentle sensitivity. And lots of prayer.

Divine Secret 4: Allow for Future Productivity

When a parent is ready to accept it, there is another "divine secret." After Ava's mom had taken a year in processing her grief quietly, she was ready to be reintegrated into family life and take on meaningful tasks again.

"One of the best things for Mom was getting her back on the organ at church. Another was doing small tasks for us—like calling AMVETS for a pickup or sending her on a mission to find our niece and nephew's Christmas gifts (they're getting a doll house and a train set). These tasks get her excited. She is contributing, and she is valued. You know, she has a lot to add. We wanted her to have a life again. And now she does. We just couldn't rush it."

Similarly, Marlee's mother, the pink-haired grandma from chapter 2, found meaningful work at her senior center, where she volunteers two days a week. After seeing her husband through a long illness, experiencing widowhood, and seeing her sisters and other extended family members die, Marlee's mom has chosen to celebrate the fact that she's still alive by serving others—rather than wallowing in survivor guilt. She's decided to *live* as long as she's living.

Pastor's wife Karen Smith told me about a ninety-one-year-old woman she visits: "She volunteered to help with the children's work at church. She is going to help with the four-year-olds every other month [giggle]—because there was an appeal from Colin from the pulpit, you see; they really needed these workers. I think that's lovely."

Divine Secret 5: Locate New, Old Friends

This secret is also about reintegrating into life. Where the previous secret was about finding meaningful service, this is about finding meaningful relationship. It can be with long-time friends who close ranks to fill gaps left by mutual loved ones gone. Or it can be with newfound friends who share a generic camaraderie of loss.

When Alice moved her mom across the country into an assisted-living facility, she felt guilty about taking her mom from her old support network. Although she seldom hears from old-home friends, Alice's mom is building new relationships. Alice chuckles as she explains, "I am proud of how Mom is adjusting. She is a caring, positive person. Now she has a 'girl' friend and a 'gentleman' friend, both at the assisted-living facility. Mom is only eighty-three, and her gentleman friend and girlfriend are ninety-five and ninety-six."

But, as the saying goes, there's nothing like *old* friends. Knowing this, psychologist Jennifer Thomas suggests adult children help parents reconnect with friends from days gone by. "Get them in touch with old friends who remember their shared history. They'll remember your parents and tell old stories together." She suggests going online to alumni websites or sites for ministries your parents participated in to help facilitate their reconnections.

This isn't always something a parent wants, though. Olivia is disappointed that her mom, never a social person, won't go on the senior bus to meet new people and enjoy new outings. But Olivia does note, "Mom has a few friends still in her home state. Yet she is reluctant to return their phone calls. I feel she needs that interaction. After she has spoken with them she is more lively—there is a sparkle in her eyes—because she has someone else to think about."

Divine Secret 6: Some Things Never Change

For our last "divine secret" let me restate an obvious truth: despite the reality of death and suffering and deterioration and change—one thing never changes. God's love for us and the presence of His family on earth to support and encourage us remain the same. We can count on God to be as He always was. "I the Lord do not change," God announces in Malachi 3:6.

The presence of His church on this earth is unchanged, as well. The analogies of the body of Christ and the family of God are as relevant today as ever. The connection in this eternal family transcends the losses our parents—or we—will experience.

Pastor Colin told me this about his parents who are in Scotland. "There are folks who contribute as spiritual family four thousand miles away. They build value into my parents' lives, and my parents in turn minister to others. The family isn't isolated. It is extended through the family of God."

Closing **Prayer**

God, would You give my grieving parent Your solid foundation, Your loving arms and tender care, as she faces change and loss. Equip me to help her process pain—but more than that, give her opportunities to connect with people and service that will make her feel productive.

Take *Action*

1. Research grief support groups in your community. See that any group you recommend is likely to be compatible with your parent's needs.

2. Locate websites of organizations or educational institutions your parent participated in earlier. Help her reconnect with friends from these or other social groups.

3. Offer ways your parent can interact in meaningful relationship with your household.

4. If your parent isn't responsive to drawing out of his grief, make time to listen to him—or be silent in grief together.

Chapter Nine

HE'S FALLEN
and He Can't Get Up

Making life safe for parents

who choose to live alone

Joy's Mom (Julie's Gram) Stays Home

Dad died when Mom was still vibrant and active. She was barely seventy, and had a lot of living yet to do. Together we decided she'd stay in her two-story home one block from ours and keep driving the two-mile-long sedan Dad had bought just before he died. She was contented, spending many days out for lunch or away on car trips with girlfriends—seldom spending any one full day at home.

But eight years into that arrangement, she admitted that she'd fallen down her staircase and asked if we could make it possible for her to stay on the main floor. John, my husband, hired a contractor to retrofit her family room with bi-fold doors (for privacy), and we bought a daybed to place along one wall in that room. This gave her access to the kitchen, a bathroom, and the living, dining, and laundry rooms. Again she was safe. John or I would go up to the second floor to be sure everything was okay—but Mom stayed downstairs.

About that time, we remodeled our home, making a place for Mom to be with us with a private bedroom/bathroom suite. But she wanted no part of it. Finally, we put her house on the market. When we found a buyer, we moved her into a new two-bedroom condo, minutes from our house—still in her familiar neighborhood. She could drive to the same stores, lunch in her old haunts, and have access to her friends—but in this elevator building, there would be no more stairs to contend with. Because of the size of her garage space in the condo, we had to trade her big sedan for Julie's compact car—but she was thrilled to keep her freedom.

This worked well until Mom reached eighty-five, when she realized she had fallen asleep at a red light on the way to church. She didn't want to hurt anyone, so she voluntarily relinquished her driver's license.

Around that time we noticed burns on Mom's arm and bruises on her legs. When we pressed her about them, she admitted she'd burned herself on the oven and she'd fallen when a throw rug in her kitchen slid. After buying her a cane, which she refused to use, we went through the condo and removed all the throw rugs. We also bought her a toaster oven, which became our annual Christmas present, because she'd burn one out every year. This allowed her to cook with less risk of burning herself.

Again, we wanted her to move in with us, but she wouldn't hear of it. John, Julie, and I began taking her shopping, running her errands, and eventually doing all her shopping for her. We'd go down the aisles of our warehouse club with three carts mounded high (one cart each for Julie and me, and the basket of John's motorized scooter for overflow)—and people would stare. But Mom, a product of the Great Depression, always had to be sure she had plenty of necessities on hand—for winter, just in case. When she died, we found stockpiles of toilet paper, laundry detergent, paper napkins, and bottled water in closets, her storeroom, even the tub in her guest bathroom.

Her greatest fear was losing her independence—and I guess it's a blessing that she never did. Mom ended up passing away after a twenty-four-hour hospitalization. She got her wish—to move right from her own home up to heaven.

MY GRAM WASN'T ALONE in her quest for independence and her desire to keep her habits and patterns by living on her own. It's called "aging in place." According to a feature story in *US News and World Report*, "The vast majority of Americans . . . grow old in their own communities. 'People want to be where their family and friends are,' says Elinor Ginzler, director of livable communities for AARP."

The *US News* article continues, "New programs, services, and technology are helping people to stay in their homes longer. Federal and state lawmakers are shifting funds from nursing homes to home- and community-based health services." The struggle, though, for adult children of independence-minded parents, is finding "a living situation that gives parents the assistance they need and the independence they desire."[15]

Never Alone

Barbara faced this dilemma with her fiercely independent, widowed mother—and came up with a viable solution. You'll recall that Barbara's mother took a fall in her bedroom and suffered injuries that required hospitalization and an extended nursing home stay. After many months she recovered well enough to return home—just not alone.

Barbara wanted her mother to move into her condo, but it wasn't a viable option, because Barbara's work would leave her mom home alone for nine hours a day. Barbara's sister was in the same situation. So the family hired an in-home caregiver. They involved their mother in the interview process. In fact, Barbara recalls, "Mom wanted us to take the lead in the interviews. But once the conversation got going, she would come up with a lot of questions for the potential caregiver."

Barbara continues to be involved as her mom's primary family caregiver—visiting often, talking by phone several times every day, doing all the grocery shopping, and having her mother at her condo every Saturday night through Sunday, when the caregiver has her day off. It wasn't easy for Barbara's mother to agree to have a stranger live with her 24/7, but it was preferable to remaining in a nursing facility.

Yet the frequency and intensity of care she requires isn't necessary for everyone. As *US News* reported, many options exist, including local programs that provide services to seniors such as "a weekly ride to the grocery store, nearby exercise classes, and access to a geriatric care manager." Other options include "a concierge service" where a program organizer screens providers of such services as plumbing, household repair, home-health nurses, social workers, heating maintenance, even routine car maintenance. These programs vary by locale, but they're growing in availability.

Safety First

One of the biggest issues for seniors who choose "aging in place" is in-home safety. They may feel as fit as when they were forty, but the reality is their bones are more brittle, muscles less flexible, and balance less sure. Where it may be tempting for them to continue climbing ladders to change lightbulbs or reach items on top shelves, it could prove dangerous.

It may be difficult to convince them of this, though, as Marie discovered with her dad, a recent widower who lives alone a few miles from each of his four children. "My brother handles outside Dad's house—snow removal, cleaning gutters, weatherizing windows. But Dad doesn't realize the extent of his medical history. His heart cannot be repaired much more." Often, she'll find her dad outside trying to do the gardening and other heavy outdoor tasks he has done for years. He is offended when she reminds him of his limitations. But because it is a matter of life and death, she doesn't worry about offending (although she does *remind* sweetly). His safety comes first.

Even beyond saving our parents from their youthful good intentions, there are many things we can do to make them safer at home.

Kitchen Safety. As we discovered with Gram, area rugs and throw rugs can be a major fall hazard. Removing them is a good first step. Eliminating other hazards, like extension cords strung across walk paths or leaky fixtures that leave slippery puddles on floors, also can help.

Bathroom Safety. Another great idea that gives maximum benefit for minimal expenditure is installing grab bars in bathrooms. This provides something safe to hold as they enter or exit a tub or shower. Suggesting they only use a shower stall or walk-in tub is wise, as well.

Portable Telephones. Years ago we gave Gram a portable telephone to carry throughout her condo. But because her hearing was bad, and the model we purchased didn't have a volume booster, she stopped using it. In the months before she died, Mom and I had discussed getting an emergency cell phone for Gram to clip to her belt or apron. We hesitated only because we knew she wouldn't remember to charge the battery, so it might be useless in a true emergency.

Personal Emergency Response Systems. Star Trek comm badges, move over. Today's technology allows two-way communication from tiny devices that can allow our loved ones to summon help at the touch of a button. If we can set aside our preconceptions and jokes we've heard about the line "I've fallen, and I can't get up," one of these systems may provide peace of mind.

Many companies have entered the market with these Personal Emergency Response Systems (PERS). Some are tied into household alarms. Others are tied into the person's medical history. They all are simple to use and work with standard telephone lines. According to *Chicago CAREgiver* magazine, "A typical PERS has three components: a small radio transmitter in the form of a help button that is carried or worn by the user; a console connected to the user's telephone; and an emergency response center that monitors calls."[16] The transmitters are worn on a neck chain or wristband.

Even for those who don't live alone, but spend part of each day alone, these units can mean the difference between immediate assistance and waiting for hours before someone finds them.

Medication Safety. Here's one final word about in-home safety. Most seniors take several—to dozens—of medications every day. The timing and dosages, while crucial to ongoing health, may be complicated and confusing, even for the sharpest parent. Having someone dispense and double-check a parent's meds is important.

In-home Visits from the Pros

But perhaps your parent is midway on the continuum between needing 24/7 help and total day-to-day independence. There are other options for in-home care. Some services offer paid helpers to come into a senior's home for an hour or two, once or twice a week.

Jennie is such a caregiver. Her skills include a compassionate heart, a willingness to do household tasks (such as laundry, light housework, and grocery shopping), and a cheery disposition. The agency for whom Jennie works hired her on the spot because they heard in her voice what bore out in her actions—that she genuinely cares. In her clients' homes, the service Jennie provides transcends the physical and moves into friendship, companionship, and encouragement.

Many companies provide nonmedical care like Jennie's. But even more medical home-care options are emerging across the country. Nurses and other trained medical professionals can visit to monitor vital signs, administer medications, and provide wound care.

But nurses aren't the only ones making house calls. Many doctors are making house calls on homebound, elderly patients—but they're now equipped with portable X-ray and ultrasound machines, blood testing facilities, and more—all housed in mobile labs that look like run-of-the-mill minivans. In 1993 Dr. Thomas Cornwell began a practice that specializes in this kind of care. Since then, he and his assistant have made more than twenty thousand house calls in the doctor's souped-up medical minivan.

Practices like Dr. Cornwell's are springing up across the country. According to the American Academy of Home Care Physicians "House Call Fact Sheet," the benefits of home care are vast:

* House calls allow the physician to become better able to interact with the patient, family, and caregivers by evaluating patients in their natural environment and developing a more comprehensive sense of physical and psychosocial needs.
* Today medical technology can increase the home health options for direct care and monitoring of patient progress.

Many of the services Dr. Cornwell and others offer, if deemed medically necessary, are covered by a patient's private insurance or Medicare/Medicaid plans, making it a viable option for many.

Loneliness for Seniors

Marie's family has found that loneliness can be the biggest downside to allowing our parents the privilege of remaining in their homes without full-time caregivers. So she and her siblings came up with a way to help combat this: every day her brother uses his lunch hour to visit and prepare lunch for their dad. This gives the elder man companionship and the family the assurance Dad is taking his medications and is doing well that day.

Churches, too, are seeing the opportunity to help combat senior loneliness in the name of Christ. In chapter 17 we'll hear about many ways churches are reaching out to the elderly, but one program warrants mention here. First Baptist Church at the Mall, Lakeland, Florida, holds special meetings the first and third Thursday evenings of every month for seniors who live alone. They draw more than a hundred people to these entertaining, dining, and socializing events, which feature a closing Scripture and salvation prayer. The church's motivation is that "as seniors find hope and spiritual solace in the company of other seniors, the church body seeks to give back to its ministry veterans, some who've been serving the church for 40 or 50 years."[17]

But for the believer in Christ, *alone* isn't truly alone. Remember Jesus' reassuring words to His followers hours before He went to the cross: "Listen to me; a time is coming when you will be scattered, each to his own home. That time is now here. *You will leave me alone, but I am never really alone, because the Father is with me*" (John 16:32 NCV, emphasis mine).

The fact of God's constant presence with our loved ones, especially with those who have lived a lifetime of faith in Him, can bring comfort to us and to them. No matter what precautions we take, we can never be 100 percent there for them and they can never be 100 percent safe, this side of eternity. But the fact that Jesus promised "I will never leave you nor forsake you" (Hebrews 13:5 NKJV) is a priceless benefit we can be sure He will deliver.

Closing **Prayer**

We'll draw today's closing prayer from *The Book of Common Prayer*, a prayer for the aged:

Look with mercy, O God our Father, on all whose increasing years bring them weakness, distress, or isolation. Provide for them homes of dignity and peace; give them understanding helpers, and the willingness to accept help; and, as their strength diminishes, increase their faith and their assurance of Your love. This we ask in the name of Jesus Christ our Lord. Amen.

Take *Action*

1. Check into options for Personal Emergency Response Systems for a parent living alone or in your home.

2. Go through your parent's living environment looking for dangers—leaky faucets, throw rugs, and extension cords—and remove them.

3. Search catalogs like *Active and Able: Daily Living Made Easier* (www.activeandable.com) to find products to make living at home safer.

4. Look for ways to alleviate the loneliness your senior parent may feel. A brief visit from a grandchild, a daily telephone call, a meal brought in by a friend—all can help break the monotony.

Chapter Ten

GUESS WHO'S
Coming to Dinner

When your parent comes to stay

Samantha Registers a Healthy Shock

*M*y *sister Ava and I sold our condo after our dad died. Together with our mother, we bought a bigger place in a new neighborhood, where all three of us could have our own space but still look out for each other.*

While Mom had been actively out and about with Dad every day of their retirement and more than fifty-year marriage, my sister and I had been working at our careers. Long ago, we'd gotten used to having a maid service clean our condo. Sure, we'd keep things picked up, but if we spent time on the heavy cleaning on our one day off, we wouldn't have enough energy left to dote on our niece and nephew—the joys of our life. When we moved, we kept up the cleaning service and added a grocery delivery service (where we order online and have our favorite items arrive at our door at a prescribed time). We didn't want our arthritic Mom schlepping groceries for three adults out of her sedan's trunk and up the steps into the kitchen every week.

Ava and I thought we were making life easier on Mom. What we didn't realize was that all these conveniences were having the opposite effect. It wasn't until Ava had to undergo surgery that would require a three-week recovery at home that it all began to make sense. At Ava's preop exam our longtime family doctor took me aside and said, "Look at that smile on your mom's face. She's thriving on this."

I'm sure my face registered abject shock. I mean, seeing my sister in such intense pain that no pill could come close to taking the edge off it was killing me. I couldn't get my mind around the idea that our sweet, godly mom could in some alternate universe be enjoying this. The doctor must have picked up on my horror, because he quickly explained, "She can't wait to have her little birdie back in the nest needing her care. She needs to feel needed."

From that day on, Ava and I started looking for ways to help Mom feel useful—to do things she loves to do, things that make a difference in other people's lives, and especially things that make an eternal difference. We definitely don't want to dump our responsibilities on her—but we do want to do everything we can to help Mom find purpose and fulfillment in this new season of her life.

THE TEASER SCREAMED ACROSS my computer screen— RETIREES LEAVE FLA. Since it fell into the man-bites-dog category of surprising news and piqued my curiosity, I followed the link. It led to a MarketWatch article headlined, "Florida's Sparking Reverse Migration." Financial journalist Robert Powell explained his parents are among the new trend of "counterstream migrants" leaving the Sunbelt. Powell wrote, "For every 1,000 people age 65 and older who 'retire' to Florida, there are about 481 who leave" to "return to their places of origin due largely to increased frailty."[18]

Apparently, the panacea of snowbird heaven is only heavenly as long as seniors are healthy enough to remain self-sufficient. But when frailty begins to chip away at independence, many parents wisely realize being near family is preferable to 80-degree, sunny winter days alone.

The "places of origin" to which counter-migrants return tend to be near—and often *with*—adult children. And they're not the only ones coming to dinner with their kids for good. Even seniors who never left familiar surroundings are moving in. *US News & World Report* calls them "boomerang parents," saying, "Forget kids who head straight from college to their old bedrooms. Out of 36 million people age 65 or older, about 13 percent live with their adult children or other family members. But the older generation requires a lot more hand-holding."[19]

All of which raises a kettle full of issues within the households of parents, host children, and their non-host siblings.

The Decision

For Ava and Samantha, the decision to have their mother live with them came before their father died. "Before Dad got sick, we were thinking someday we would sell the two properties and get one big one together. As they got older, we knew they would need help. Then, when he knew he was dying, Dad asked Samantha and me to promise him we would take care of our mother," Ava recalls.

Their brother was on board with the decision, as he was preparing for his retirement out of state. The two condos sold, and the three women joined households. When their brother moved southwest with his wife, he bought a home with a guest room where Mom could spend extended visits—if only they could get her to swallow her fears and board an airplane.

But not all families amicably agree on arrangements. For one thing, there are financial considerations. How much of the parents' finances go into the purchase or retrofitting of the home? How are everyday expenses handled? For what expenses or errands are other siblings responsible? What happens to the home and the finances once the parent dies or moves into a care facility? With complex financial decisions like these, family disharmony may be an unwelcome byproduct.

When Ann and her husband built a home that included an in-law apartment for Ann's mother, Beatrice, Ann was concerned about how her siblings (one sister and four brothers) would respond. "I've been handling Mom and Dad's finances for a long time [her dad died while the home was being built], so I didn't want misunderstandings with my sister and brothers. I asked my brothers to draw up a contract."

They wrote a contract that arranged for Beatrice to contribute money toward the building project. They decided Ann would "repay" that money by caring for their mother. For each of the first ten years, Ann would "earn" a tenth of the money their mom put into the house. "After ten years, it would be taken care of," she says. The family is six years into the arrangement, and all parties are content with its fairness.

Christian financial advisor Ron Blue recommends: "It's best to have all the affected people in the room together. It can be a difficult situation—a lot of people cannot deal with it emotionally. In these cases, you may get a facilitator, a financial planner or accountant who has done it before . . . someone who can integrate biblical wisdom into the advice and counsel." Blue's organization: www.kingdomadvisors.com offers referrals to biblical financial experts.

The Big "C"–Compromise

But even once financial considerations are ironed out, the kettle is full of issues that will affect the transition.

In one sense, Samantha and Ava's situation was ideal, in that the three moved into a neutral location on equal footing—it was no one's home "first"; it was theirs together. But to make it work, Ava says the biggest key was "compromise."

For example, their mom's condo had been decorated in neutral beige and 1980s blue. They decided each woman could bring a few favorite pieces to the home—especially to decorate her bedroom and bathroom—but the daughters wanted the common areas to be contemporary and vibrant. When they went furniture shopping together, their mom was drawn to all things beige—frustrating the daughters. Finally, Mom walked up to a sofa, sat down, and said, "This is the one."

It was, amazingly, wine-red—a color all three love. "We wanted to know who she was and what she had done with our mother," Ava says.

The compromise continues with little issues like how warm to keep the house (Mom is always hot), who gets the inside parking spaces (they have three cars and two garage stalls), and who does the cooking (Samantha is a gourmet cook, but Mom is home all day and is anxious to be useful). There is no debate on the kitchen cleanup, though. That's Ava's job.

Overall, it is working. Ava admits, "If we hadn't moved in together, we'd have had to be at Mom's condo every day, constantly checking on her."

Likewise, Ann and Beatrice are friends as well as mother and daughter. But even friends need their space. Their cooking habits are different, so each woman has her own kitchen. And their temperaments are different, so they've worked out an arrangement. Ann explains, "I live my life on the edge, always running. When I come home, I need peace and quiet. But Mom has been alone all day and when she hears my footsteps upstairs, she needs to talk. We worked out an understanding. If I come to her kitchen and keep standing, we are not going to talk long. If I sit down, we can talk longer."

Beatrice understands this signal and respects her daughter's needs. But she adds, "Nobody knows how I feel when I hear her footsteps upstairs—it is wonderful!"

Retrofitting a Home

Samantha, Ava, and Ann have ideal situations with their mom being youthful, mobile, and healthy. But not all adult children of boomerang parents are so blessed. For government employee Dean, his mother's deteriorating health and his sister's burnout after fifteen years of live-in caregiving precipitated a cross-country move for his household (his wife and teenage children)—and building a new home that would be handicap accessible.

The first consideration was a home where every family member could be comfortable. They settled on a tri-level with Grandma on the lowest level, common areas on the middle level, and the upper level that houses bedrooms and a TV room. This allows a "buffer zone" so the noise of the kids or of Grandma's blaring TV doesn't disturb the others.

But a multilevel home wasn't the best for an elder adult with limited mobility, so the family installed a lift from Grandma's zone onto the main floor.

Dean was conscious of his mom's needs in more than the big-picture design. He installed a RadioShack intercom throughout the house. (Our family has the same system—it can be installed in multiple rooms, wherever a telephone jack is present.) Additionally, he uses a Life Alert personal emergency response system, which his mom wears in case of emergencies when the family is at work and school.

He made other adaptations as well:

One of the big things is clearing a path around the furniture so she can get around safely in her wheelchair. We have grab bars in the bathroom, a ramp to get into the house, and a recliner that raises to lift her. In her kitchen, we gave her a smaller table on wheels that she can bring to the recliner. We made room under the sinks for her wheelchair. We lowered the thermostat, light switches, even her two-burner stove. We put electrical outlets higher, so she can reach them from her chair.

These adaptations allow Dean's mother independence and safety.

Move-in During Crisis

Dean had time to plan for his mother's transition. But other adult children don't have that luxury. Frances moved her mom into her home during the last stages of her mom's battle with lung cancer.

Mom was too ill to make it up the three flights of stairs to her and Dad's senior citizen apartment. Dad decided to stay in the apartment, and Mom came to live with me. Dad came to be with her during the day; then he went home at night when my husband and I were home.

A friend let us borrow a hospital bed she had. So we set it up for mom in one of our bedrooms. But until the last week of her life, Mom didn't use that bed—she could breathe better on the sofa, sitting up.

As Frances demonstrates, even in crisis times, there are ways to make quick adjustments that can make ailing parents comfortable and welcome. There are catalogs of products that range from large-button telephones and clocks, to talking scales, magnifiers, ergonomic grippers and openers, toilet safety supports, bed rails, lift chairs, medication dispensers, and more that can make living in your home or theirs safer.

The Value of Relationship

But it isn't all challenges when Grandma or Grandpa comes to dinner to stay. Part of keeping a multigenerational household operating smoothly stems from the value of relationship—especially when all the members share a faith in Christ.

The *Women's Study Bible* lists ways a grandparent can be a benefit in the home. These include talking about the grandparent's salvation experience, praying with grandchildren, reading the Bible together, and showing them they are important to God and He is in control of everyday circumstances.[20]

This is something Holly and Bridget recall fondly from their growing-up years in their grandmother's company. Before she succumbed to dementia, their grandma was babysitter, confidante, and friend. "She would play any game we wanted to play," Holly recalls.

Bridget says, "I liked to play jewelry store with all her costume jewelry."

But the fun didn't stop with games. "She would write Scripture verses on pieces of paper, and we would memorize them together," Bridget says.

Holly adds, "Grandma never forgot Jesus. Even in the last six months when she couldn't read the Bible anymore, she would talk about Jesus."

A Model to Follow

Families like those who've shared their live-in stories in this chapter and those in the previous chapter who have seen to their parents' care in special, thoughtful ways model a trait that would please the Lord—honor and respect for elder family members.

Consider one of the phrases we call the seven last words of Christ—spoken from His cross. John 19:26–27 reports: "When Jesus saw his mother there, and the disciple whom he loved standing nearby, he said to his mother, 'Dear woman, here is your son,' and to the disciple, 'Here is your mother.' From that time on, this disciple took her into his home."

Commentator Matthew Henry says of this tender scene,

[Jesus'] mother, perhaps, was so taken up with his sufferings that she thought not of what would become of her; but he admitted that thought. Silver and gold he had none to leave, no estate, real or personal; his clothes the soldiers had seized. . . . He had therefore no other way to provide for his mother than by his interest in a friend, which he does here.

Imagine our Lord seeing to the care of His mother even in the moment of His unspeakable suffering. It may be a sacrifice that calls for compromise and inconvenience to bring an ailing loved one into our home (or care for him in his own home)—but it is one we can consider part of our service to the Lord.

Recall the words Paul wrote to the Colossians: "Whatever you do, work at it with all your heart, as working for the Lord, not for men" (Colossians 3:23). The thoughts beside that verse in the *Believer's Bible Commentary* include this statement, "The humblest service can be glorified and dignified by doing it for the Lord. . . . Rewards in heaven will not be for prominence or apparent successes; they will not be for talents or opportunities; but rather for faithfulness. Thus obscure persons will fare very well in that day if they have carried out their duties faithfully as to the Lord."

Closing Prayer

God, thank You for the privilege of coming alongside my parent and for the home You've given me that I can open to her. Help us through the challenges of transitioning her into our home—and give us grace and reassurance that we are doing this in Your strength, for Your glory.

Take *Action*

1. If your parent is no longer safe or happy living alone, convene a family meeting to discuss options.

2. Examine your parent's future surroundings to be sure you've taken every precaution for her ongoing safety. Check online to find senior safety products.

3. Discuss ways to make your parent feel "at home" and useful. Suggest ways he can contribute to family life—spiritually or physically.

4. Give your parent the option to choose favorite items to bring into her new surroundings.

Chapter Eleven

TABLE FOR 22,
Please

Choosing an assisted-living

or nursing facility

Julie Observes a Touching Scene

My folks and I were sitting over a late lunch at our favorite upscale neighborhood pit/barbecue restaurant. Like most seniors, my folks like eating their "big meal" midday, but they'd agreed to let me work until mid-afternoon and lunch "late" (translation: 2 p.m.). It was slow in the restaurant, and the few heads bobbing in conversation at tables were white-haired.

As we were sipping our soup, I saw a young woman walk up to the hostess and ask if the restaurant could accommodate a group of twenty-two. Busboys scrambled to move tables and set up for the unexpected flurry.

The young woman walked outside, then reappeared with a strong-looking man and twenty senior citizens, residents of a local assisted-living facility. One was wheelchair bound (the strong man pushed him into place); others were handicapped—depending on canes and crutches, and leaning on each other.

I did a double-take as I realized that among the group was the first secretary I had out of graduate school. I hadn't seen her in seventeen years, and it shook me to see her aged and infirm.

After they were settled, I walked to the table and spoke to my former secretary. While she was kind, I wasn't convinced she remembered me. She asked the same question several times about a former colleague— but she didn't seem able to process my response. I returned to my seat but couldn't stop watching what was going on at that table.

The lead caregiver captured my attention. Rather than leaving the work to the restaurant's wait staff, she went to each individual, called him or her by name, and took orders—offering suggestions. "Joe, you usually drink Coke; would you like a Coke today?" "Mary, would you like coffee?" "Jim, you said you wanted a burger; you usually want them medium well. Is that how you'd like it today?" "Anna, would you like your sweater so you don't get cold?"

During the meal, this caregiver offered help, sugar packets, an extra napkin, whatever was called for. All the while her salad sat untouched at her place. One male dementia patient was more than a little too touchy-feely with her, but she didn't even wince. Her patience, her gracious spirit, her attentiveness to her elder charges spoke well of the facility that employs her.

As we were leaving, I said good-bye to my former secretary and tapped the caregiver on the shoulder. "I hope when I need care, I have a caregiver half as kind and attentive as you are," I whispered in her ear. She grinned and reached across the table to stop a glass of Coke from spilling on one of her elder charges.

WHEN I WAS LITTLE, I loved singing solos in church. I was still young when Bill and Gloria Gaither premiered their song "I Am Loved" at a concert at Chicago's Arie Crown Theater. The song touched my heart, and I bought the music so I could sing it in my grandfather's church.

During the following summer vacation, my mom's friend was

conducting services at a nearby nursing home. She invited Mom to play the piano and me to sing.

That day is a jumble of sensory images: the pungent odor of soiled diapers and ammonia. The dazed looks of crumpled people, buried under stained, knobby blankets and slouched in wheelchairs in a multipurpose room with peeling wallpaper (who chooses these patterns?) and scuffed flooring. Disinterested staffers, loitering in the shadows. The twangs and tings of the dilapidated piano Mom played as I sang that Gaither song.

I'm not sure why, but when I got to the line "I am loved, you are loved/won't you please take my hand?" I walked among the wheelchairs and started taking residents' hands—looking them in the eye and feeling them squeeze my hand back. I had held hands with every resident by the time it was over, and the strangest thing happened: The audience came awake as I passed by, made alert because of the touch of my hand.

Several things happened in me that day. First, I began to understand the power of a gentle touch. Second, I knew God loved those folks in that room—and the plan of salvation was as much for them at their stage of life as it was for me at mine. And finally, I knew I never, ever wanted to see one of my loved ones abandoned in a place that smelled as repulsive and felt as hopeless as that room had before the love of God invaded it.

Some Definitions

Fortunately, elder care has come a long way in the thirty-plus years since that scene. Not only are nursing homes more regulated (due to the Omnibus Budget Reconciliation Act of 1987 that set federal standards of care), but there are more options available today. *Medical News Today* says,

* "Over the past 20 years, there has been a significant decline away from nursing home settings, particularly among the 'oldest old'—persons 85 and older."

* "Less disability can mean fewer people in nursing homes, and higher income provides the freedom to exercise more choice and pay for services in the community."

* "Because of changes in Medicare reimbursement and other forces, nursing homes increasingly focus on post-acute rehabilitation."[21]

Since we've already discussed rehab and in-home care, we'll turn our attention to assisted-living and nursing facilities. Let's begin with a definition. According to the website of the American Academy of Home Care Physicians,

"Assisted living" (AL) or "housing with services" has become increasingly popular, with approximately 800,000 elderly residing in over 30,000 such facilities in the U.S. These buildings typically offer a meal program, housekeeping, activities, and some level of nursing services on site.

Most AL programs are designed to provide long-term supportive care to chronically, but not acutely, ill elderly. . . . Assisted living programs seek to enable the frail elderly to avoid nursing home placement.

The men and women I observed eating with their caregivers were certainly frail—a generation ago they might have lost their independence prematurely to a nursing home. But assisted living allows them to be mobile enough to board a handicap-accessible bus and have an outing in the community.

Personalizing Her Space

Another benefit of assisted living is that the elder can bring personal items to furnish his small, private apartment. Having familiar items around makes it feel home-like and comfortable.

Yet, the freedom of assisted living does not come at the expense of personal safety, as residents receive professional, managed care and assistance with daily tasks. Since it doesn't carry negative associations that nursing care may hold, parents who qualify for it may be more willing to entertain the possibility of making this transition.

Nursing-home chaplain Dale Sawyer sees these situations every day, and he's lived them with his in-laws. In convincing them to move to a retirement community, the chaplain told them, "You're going to find new friends there." He talked about playing dominoes with new friends, going to Bible study, knitting, swimming, and exercises—all things they would enjoy.

Is It Time?

So far, we've hinted at the emotional minefield involved. But it's a topic that can't be ignored. Experts suggest that to minimize emotional upset we have candid discussions with our parents regarding their wishes. Eliciting a parent's input before the heat of a situation can be a great guide. However, there is a difference between knowing someone's preferences and being able to meet her expectations in a crisis. Marcy offers this caution:

I made Mom a promise that I'd never put her in a nursing home. But eventually, after she had fallen and broken her ribs, I had to go back on my word. I felt tremendous guilt about this. But with her injuries, her dementia, and the cancer that was ravaging her body, we couldn't care for her at home. I was mentally numb and exhausted, which isn't the greatest time to make a major decision. Even though I knew it was best, it was the hardest decision I ever had to make, because I knew I was going against my word and her wishes.

For Marcy's mom, assisted living was no option, because she required constant medical attention. This is a major criterion in the decision between assisted living and nursing care. Chaplain Sawyer says it's time to consider these options when "family members cannot handle the health issues or the mental issues."

While there are few hard-and-fast rules on when a nursing home is the best option, the following definition is helpful:

Nursing homes provide care for people whose medical needs require the attention of licensed nurses, but not the more intensive care of a hospital. Admission requires a doctor's order. Nurse's aides provide much of the day-to-day care. Social workers and case managers help seniors and their families with insurance issues and the coordination of nursing care plans. Dietitians, physical and occupational therapists and other health professionals help support and sustain seniors' physical and emotional well-being.[22]

Because nursing-home admission requires a doctor's order, it's not a decision we're left to on our own. According to www.myziva.net, "You can speak with the hospital discharge planner, who can suggest several nursing homes that may meet your needs. Elder care lawyers, your doctor, clergy, ombudsman, the Department of Social Services and your local library can be very helpful."

Evaluating a Facility

When it comes time to choose a facility, there is no shortage of counsel. Chaplain Sawyer suggests considering:

* quality of medical attention
* attractiveness of the environment
* whether it is well kept, bright, and clean
* one-on-one contact with staff
* whether it is owned by a not-for-profit or profit-making corporation
* whether it offers a Christ-centered environment
* the family's ability to pay for this level of service

MyZiva.net lists a family -member's "gut" feeling as one key criterion. This website offers facility comparisons according to objective measures like government inspections, ratio of patients to medical staff, reports of harm to patients, and more.

However, a facility may not necessarily accept your parent. When Laura was looking for an assisted-living situation for her mother-in-law, she found "some facilities had guidelines about what a resident could do for herself, and she didn't qualify." In the end, Laura is "pleased with the quality and attentiveness" of the staff at the faith-based facility that did accept her mother-in-law. "There is a doctor there and twenty-four-hour nursing care." That's the level of care the family knew Mom would need. But because they realize her situation could deteriorate, they made sure the facility could handle additional challenges.

In looking for a facility, experts suggest a family be ready to:

Explain the type of care your loved one needs. Ask the facility to describe how it will meet those needs, for example, assistance with dressing, taking medications, incontinence, or general supervision. A nursing home should provide enough care and support to meet your loved one's needs while encouraging and allowing them to remain as independent as possible.[23]

When moving her mother across country, Alice became a mini-expert in assisted living. She found forty options in her area, so she began with those closest to her home, and sought a place with an Alzheimer's unit (her mom was experiencing memory loss), so "we wouldn't have to switch later." She talked to her city's "assisted-living ombudsman"—an expert on all the facilities she was considering. She asked, "If it were your mom, where would you place her?"

She visited one place he suggested that felt oppressive to her. "I went out to my car and cried. There were just a lot of people sitting around staring."

But she knew when she had found the right place—it was bright and cheery, and the staff made her feel confident. "My mom wanted to be on the first floor—to look out over grass." The room she wanted opened up: "It was a total God-thing," Alice says. "She is down the hall from the living room, dining room, and all the activities. She loves the food—and having someone to eat with for all her meals."

Alice reflects,

It was a tremendous amount of work to choose a facility, deal with all the paperwork, get Mom moved across the country, and get her settled. She was apprehensive, and my sister and I were stressed! But within a few weeks of moving, she told me, "I feel better than I've felt in a long time." That made it all worth it. My sister and I are happy to see Mom in a beautiful home, surrounded by people she enjoys, and with medical care and other help available nearby at the touch of a button.

Paying the Bills

While finding the financing for ongoing care is beyond the scope of this book, it does warrant a few words.

First, other than brief post-hospitalization stays in rehab, Medicare doesn't pay for long-term living in either kind of facility. Neither do most health insurance plans. So, unless your parent has long-term care insurance, financing will either be through your parent's resources or Medicaid (if your parent's assets and income are low enough). A financial adviser can provide specific counsel.

The other issue is that once we know a parent's resources, the challenge is to look for the best care she can realistically afford. Laura says the situation her family chose "was expensive, but we worked with Mom's bank on her investments" to make the best estimate of the care she could afford for her expected lifespan. The website www.aging-parents-and-elder-care.com has a grid that estimates remaining life expectancy, to help with this calculation.

An Issue of Family and Faith

Once the decision is made and a parent is settled in, Chaplain Sawyer says the worst thing a family can do is stay away. Marcy didn't allow guilt to keep her away. She and other family members visited her mom daily—took her to the facility's worship services, wheeled her to meals, combed her hair, and provided other services.

The chaplain also suggests families incorporate the parent into holidays, birthdays, and family events. Alice does this—and relishes the fact that little Amy will have memories of her grandma. Amy loves her grandma, and her grandma lights up whenever Amy is near.

As Amy's hugs make her grandma's day, so "a touch on the shoulder, even a hug" can reinvigorate a resident, Chaplain Sawyer says. That may be why so many residents responded warmly to my little "I Am Loved" hand-holding song.

The chaplain takes teddy bears into Alzheimer's wards, as part of his ministry. "I find a lot of women—and even some men—love to hold the bears. There is something warm and cuddly about them." He says these methods help residents recognize him and listen to his brief devotions and gospel messages.

He offers devotions, prayer, communion, and a compassionate ear.

He brings audio recordings of the Bible to leave with residents whose eyesight doesn't allow them to read. He attends social gatherings, performs funerals, and realizes he may be their only contact with Christian leaders. Whether it's the old bedside prayer ("Now I lay me down to sleep") or the Twenty-Third Psalm, he taps into their memories of faith—and helps equip them to enter eternity, when the time comes.

Closing **Prayer**

God, only You know the preconceptions, fears, guilt, and sadness I feel as I consider helping my parent relocate into a facility. Help me make an honest assessment of places I visit—and how my parent might be served there. Give me grace and wisdom.

Take *Action*

1. Go to http://www.aahsa.org/consumer_info/default.asp for a questionnaire to fill out with your parent about preferences regarding circumstances that might call for relocating to a facility.

2. Visit www.myziva.net for information on choosing and evaluating a nursing home.

3. Check out http://www.aahsa.org for suggestions on how to tour a nursing home.

4. If your parent is in a facility, find ways to continue participating in his life—and allow him to participate in yours.

Chapter Twelve

BRINGING
Up Baby

Hope for caregivers sandwiched

---

between aging parents

---

and small children

Holly and Bridget: Fond Memories of Grandma

W*hen our mother and father were married a little over three years, they built a home on a lake an hour outside the city where they'd grown up. It was an idyllic setting, and they wanted our widowed Grandma with them. They built her a darling "in-law" apartment in the lower level of their home, and she moved in.*

It wasn't long before the two of us came along, two years apart. Grandma was a part of our lives all through our early childhood. We never had a babysitter—because Grandma was there. She played games with us. She would take us on walks around the lake. She would tell stories about her childhood and about Mom as a little girl.

One of the things we liked best was baking with Grandma. Even more fun than sampling her treats was working beside her. We wish now we'd paid more attention. But what we remember most was that she'd give us each a little piece of dough. We'd work it until it was gray from our oily little hands—then she'd let us put it on the pan and bake it beside her masterpieces.

It was a treat for us to go "'visit" Grandma. Even though she was just downstairs, it was still going to Grandma's house, where we'd be treated like special guests.

Our great sadness came when we realized Grandma's mind was slipping away. It happened gradually, and at first we didn't realize what was going on—we were pretty young. But for the last five years of her life we knew she had dementia, probably Alzheimer's. We were so attuned to her nighttime cries that even after she died, we both kept thinking we'd hear her calling out or wandering around her apartment in the dark (she refused to use nightlights).

Mom and Dad never made us feel as if her care were our responsibility. We never felt we had to stay home on Friday nights or miss going out with friends, but we genuinely wanted to help. When we were old enough, we would force Mom and Dad to go out to dinner while we watched Grandma. They'd be back in an hour—and we'd ask, "Why didn't you stay out longer?" We would have sat with her longer so they could have a break.

We learned a lot from having Grandma in our home—like patience and sticking together as a family. Mom says we learned to think of someone other than ourselves, which is a great lesson for us to have learned as teenagers.

AS IF WE DIDN'T HAVE ENOUGH classifications and sub-classifications of generations in our culture (Boomers, Busters, Generation X . . .), here's another one for you. You may already be in it; if you are, it'll help to hear its name—an aptly chosen metaphor that probably describes exactly how you're feeling: the Sandwich Generation. It's where Marcy, Holly, and Bridget's mother found herself for most of her children's growing up years. It can bring a mix of joy and sorrow, triumphs and challenges as it plays out in your household.

According to Janet Taylor, M.D., "People most often between the ages of 35 and 55, may find themselves providing care for aging parents *and* their children under age 21. This group of people is often called 'sandwich generation' because they are wedged between dual caregiving responsibilities."[24]

Sandwiched for a Season

One woman I interviewed who fits into this generation described her life as "going from getting her children out of diapers and through adolescence to having her parents regress through adolescence and into diapers." If you're in this class of hardworking caregivers, take heart. Others in similar situations can offer suggestions about ways to avoid becoming the salami in the middle.

One way to make it easier is to realize this is but one season—a season that will change. Your household won't always be teeming with energetic toddlers; your family room won't always house a hospital bed where your aging loved one convalesces; your evenings won't always be spent in medical facilities; your teenagers won't always be clamoring for you to attend school functions or sporting matches.

It's a biblical concept identified by the wise King Solomon thousands of years ago:

There is a time for everything,
and a season for every activity under heaven:
a time to be born and a time to die,
a time to plant and a time to uproot,
a time to kill and a time to heal,
a time to tear down and a time to build,
a time to weep and a time to laugh,
a time to mourn and a time to dance. (Ecclesiastes 3:1–4)

One reason it helps to identify this as a *season* rather than a *generation* is that it's easy to feel overwhelmed when we think the situation will never resolve, the caregiving will never end. But realizing seasons do change and, as the psalmist said, "weeping may endure for a night, but joy comes in the morning" (Psalm 30:5 NKJV) can become a coping mechanism. "This, too, shall pass" can become a reassuring and comforting refrain.

Another benefit to calling this a *season* is something we observe in the Ecclesiastes quote: every season isn't made for every activity. Just as in northern climates there isn't much waterskiing going on in January or snowboarding going on in July—so, too, some seasons of life don't allow us to do everything we used to be able to do in other seasons.

It's a principle I addressed in an entire chapter of my book *Conquering the Time Factor*. But the kernel of truth boils down to this:

> People will move in and out of our lives. Bosses. Friends. Colleagues. Even family members. Our roles in their lives will be ever changing—at times we may be solely responsible for them (as with nurturing tiny tots or caring for elderly relatives). Other times they may seem not to need anything from us at all. . . . [Seasons] bring with them their own special sets of demands. . . . The tasks we expect ourselves to be able to accomplish on a regular basis in one season of life may be unattainable, even undesirable, in another season.[25]

We release ourselves from energy-draining, pointless guilt when we acknowledge this truth and live as if we understand it. In this season, we'll need to set aside our preconceptions of how we *ought* to spend our time and instead focus on seeing that the critical tasks are covered—by someone.

Shifts of Caregiving

In their caregiving season Marcy and her husband devised a creative scheme to share the responsibilities. When both had to be out of the house at once, her mother's youngest brother would telephone to talk with his sister to keep her occupied. This would calm her—and reminiscing would be great for her mood.

But as she declined, she could no longer be left alone during waking hours. To accommodate, Marcy's husband changed his work schedule to the night shift. Marcy would leave for her job as a teacher when her mom would still be asleep, leaving only a short period when she might be awake and alone. Before leaving for work, Marcy would prepare a thermos of coffee and a sandwich for her mother. Then when Marcy's husband would get home around 2:00 in the afternoon, he would prepare a meal for the two of them, and begin dinner for the family.

Their daughters recall that during the latter period of their grandma's illness the family never left the house together. Marcy decries the fact that her daughters never had both parents at tennis matches—one would drop the girls off, stay for a while, then return home so the other could catch the end of the match and drive the girls home. When it came to parent-teacher conferences, it was always one or the other parent—never both.

But shared caregiving shifts—and good planning—kept the family operating safely and lovingly for an exhausting season of two years.

How to Avoid Becoming Salami

Another way to help maintain energy and sanity in this season of competing demands is to spin off tasks others can do. We'll discuss this in chapter 15, but here it's appropriate to consider that we won't be able to do some things we'd like to do.

Psychologist and author Jennifer Thomas is a young mom. She suggests "outsourcing" to keep ourselves sane. For example, she found cooking clubs like Dream Dinners, Let's Dish, and Super Suppers (see a partial list in appendix 2) where a month of family meals can be prepared ahead and frozen.

As another example, if you can afford to have a service come once a month to do heavy-duty cleaning, that could free time for tasks only you can do. Even if you can't afford help, there may be tasks other family members can assume.

Authors Alice Domar and Laura Jana suggest, "Involve your children in the care of their grandma or grandpa, whenever possible. Small children can provide entertainment by singing and dancing and creating pictures to hang in the room. Older children can perform tasks ranging from reading aloud, to bringing in fresh water, to light housekeeping duties."[26]

Kids and Grandparents Pitching In

Even your aging parent may be able to contribute to the family's well-being. Author Nicole Levison, who participated in caregiving for her grandmother and great-grandmother, points out, "If an aging family member lives with you, encourage him or her to help with a meal or the garden, or watch TV with your kids while you make dinner. Being a part of the global picture helps people feel a sense of belonging—instead of feeling in the way!"[27]

One of the biggest contributions grandparents can make to their grandchildren is spending time together. For believers in Christ, this can be a rich time when they not only pass along recipes and traditions, but the bigger issues of faith—memorizing Scriptures together or reading Bible stories or singing Sunday school songs. I remember that my grandma, who worked in the church nursery, loved to sing the "Only a boy named David" song, telling the exploits of young warrior David from 1 Samuel 17. Now, God didn't gift her with Sandi Patty's voice. It was gravelly; it cracked and squeaked. But as the stone went up in the air—woo, woo, woo—and "the giant came tumbling down," I learned about God's personal care at Grandma's knee.

It's like Paul told Timothy: "I have been reminded of your sincere faith, which first lived in your grandmother Lois and in your mother

Eunice and, I am persuaded, now lives in you also" (2 Timothy 1:5). While each family member needs to make a faith choice on his own, passing the faith through the family tree is a boon for child and grandparent.

I see this in the story of Ruth and Naomi that we've considered from several angles. Here the relevant lesson comes in Ruth 4:13–16 when Ruth marries Boaz and the couple has a son together. We get the charming picture in verse 16: "Then Naomi took the child, laid him in her lap and cared for him." Naomi, who had considered herself used up and of no value (Ruth 1:12), now received the privilege of participating in raising her surrogate grandson—who would become grandfather to King David.

Multigenerational Laughter

Even with all these ways stress can be diffused for the salami mom, one more remains on the prescription tablet: the sound of laughter.

Sometimes when her girls were of the age when they still needed a babysitter, Marcy would leave them with her mother. It wasn't clear who was babysitting whom. Looking out for each other might be the best descriptor.

Holly and Bridget confide that their grandma "had their back," and they had hers. They'd listen to old stories again and again. They'd pretend to love her cookies even when she left out sugar or flour. "We couldn't hurt her feelings, so, we'd play along, take a bite, and say we were saving the rest for later."

She returned the favor. Before they understood dementia or had interpreted its signs, they stayed in their grandma's care while their parents were out. Holly was playing with her parents' bedroom telephone, which had a direct dial button to 911. In play, she hit the button. Minutes later, the police rang the doorbell, and Grandma answered. She vehemently defended her girls and sent the officers on their way. The girls begged her not to tell their parents, and, Holly recalls, "Grandma's bad memory came in handy that day. She never remembered to tell." It wasn't until mother and daughters were sitting around the interview table with me that the truth came out. At this distance, it was good for a big laugh.

Every family with small children and aging parents has similar stories to tell. Alice is the epitome of a sandwiched caregiver. She has a four-year-old daughter, a husband battling cancer, a teenaged stepson, and a mother in a nearby assisted-living facility. Yet, she finds sources of joy and laughter: "When I bring Amy to visit Mom, Amy just brightens up everybody's day. Amy has a hundred grandparents there—all wanting her to visit them."

So even with Mom and Dad sandwiched between two care-needy generations, the benefits of multigenerational family cooperation can counterbalance—or even outweigh—its stresses.

Closing Prayer

God, *sandwiched* describes what I'm feeling. The pressures of work and home—the distress of watching my parent become as needy as my child. These arc wearing me down. Show me how others in my household can participate in appropriate ways to make my load a little lighter. Help me find respite and joyful laughter in this pressured season.

Take *Action*

1. If your parent is able to interact with your spouse and children, make a list of the ways he can participate in family life—even if it's from a couch or hospital bed. Then ask your parent if he'd like to take on one of those tasks.

2. Create a list of fun ways your child can participate in your parent's care.

3. Explain your parent's limitations or illness to your child, in age-appropriate terms. Be prepared to answer your child's questions honestly.

4. Look for the humor in every day. It'll be there.

Chapter Thirteen

PEOPLE WHO
Need People

Asking for and finding help

in the caregiving journey

Jennie—A Heart to Care for Others' Parents

I was a medical receptionist from 1978 to 1990, when I quit to work in the office for my husband's trucking company. Now, I'm sixty years old, and I didn't think after being out of the medical field for so long I'd be able to catch up without lots of classes. Since I wanted to supplement our income, I thought of health-care giving, because I like being with older people.

Yes, I'm a paid caregiver. But I see myself doing ministry as much as providing a service for senior citizens who need some help. I guess part of my motivation is that I wish my parents were still alive so I could hug them, take care of them, take them into my home, and do whatever they might need me to do. But since they're not, I'm glad to be able to do special services for someone else's parents. For some of my clients, I come in one or two days a week, do light housekeeping, put a few loads of laundry in the washer and dryer, take them grocery shopping, and talk with them all the while.

For others who aren't able to function as well, I sit beside them and read for an hour. When I started, the organization told me I could read whatever I wanted—even a cookbook if that's what I wanted to do. But instead, I got a copy of the devotional book Names of Women of the Bible *(by Julie-Allyson Ieron), and I read a devotion to them and pray the chapter's closing prayer with them each time.*

One lady who is bedridden perks up whenever I read this book. And one day as I read, I explained the plan of salvation to her and she prayed with me to receive Christ as her Savior. I can't tell you how meaningful these times can be. My thought is, Lord, this must be Your calling on my life. It is giving me pleasure; it is rewarding to others.

I know the families of my clients care about their loved ones—but they can't be there all the time. That's why they hire me to be there. I see it as a privilege to be able to come alongside as their parents age and do something that makes their lives a little better.

WE MAY THINK OF ISOLATION in the aging process as affecting only our elders. But, as our parents' needs increase, caregivers become afflicted with the same isolation issues as our parents. Where they may be in pain or limited in movement, we (who aren't as young as we used to be) are kicking our engines into overdrive—and leaving them there too long without enough cool-down or idle time. So we spin off nonessential (and many essential) tasks—like friendships, recreational activities, self-care, nutrition, and exercise.

While we'll further address caregiver self-care in chapter 15, I raise the issue here because one crucial element is knowing when to ask for help—and keeping ourselves from feeling guilty when we do ask.

In my book *Conquering the Time Factor,* I made an attempt to blow holes in the myth that "we can do and be everything everyone in our lives needs at every moment of every day." Here's how I explained why this myth cannot be true:

Since there is one God and we are not He, it's [an expectation] we can't fulfill. When we make our futile attempts . . . we shirk our own responsibilities, misuse our own time resources, and build our frustration (or even anger) levels to fuse-blowing proportions. It can be a subtle temptation, this self-importance complex.

I recognize myself in the "frustration" and "fuse-blowing" word pictures—perhaps you see yourself, as well. When exhaustion begins to dictate our actions and attitudes, we cannot help but become irritable. "At those moments, my attitude is the farthest possible from the one Jesus modeled—one of humility, of servanthood, of self-sacrifice (rather than self-importance)." I know *self-importance* is a harsh phrase to apply to a caregiver, but when we get the idea we're the only one who can meet all our parent's physical and emotional needs, we're on our way to trying to crown ourselves god of their lives.

Seeking Help without Guilt

Olivia noticed this in caring for her mom. While we'll get her full story later, the highlights are that Olivia and her brothers realized their mom could no longer live on her own, and that it made sense to have the mom move in with Olivia. One brother lives near Olivia with his wife; the other lives two states away.

At first Olivia assumed responsibility for all her mom's needs. She soon found herself exhausted. At a blowout point, Olivia approached her brothers and asked for help. What she found was that they had been reluctant to volunteer because they didn't want her to think she wasn't fulfilling her role well.

Talk about miscommunication. She didn't want to ask. And they didn't want to offer—because they didn't want to disrespect the work she was doing. It's ironed out now—and both are lightening Olivia's load by participating in their mom's care.

Help provided by family members can be the best respite for the day-to-day caregiver. Church-based caregiver Karen Smith says caregiver and receiver usually trust another family member ahead of an outsider. She says care receivers, in particular, are suspicious of outsiders and feel uncomfortable having nonfamily members helping them with personal, private tasks.

Olivia finds this when she travels on business. When she's going to be away for more than three days at a time, her brother flies into town and spends the week with their mom. "I go away with my mind at ease that she is being well cared for. And they have a great time together."

Someone to Talk to

According to the National Institute on Aging (NIA), family caregivers with the Lone Ranger complex aren't able to provide the best care. Richard Schulz, Ph.D., reported on a caregivers study designed to "identify the most promising approaches to decrease caregiver burden and depression." Schulz says the study found these elements of caregiver support to provide a noticeable improvement in quality of care: "information sharing, instruction, role playing, problem solving, skills training, stress-management techniques and telephone support groups." He writes,

> [Caregivers] reported that taking part in the program helped them feel more confident in working with the care recipient, made life easier for them, improved their ability to care for the person . . . improved the care recipient's life, and helped them keep the patient at home.[28]

Sadly, some of the guilt that keeps us from asking for help can come from a misinterpretation of a directive written by Paul: "If any widow has children or grandchildren, let them first learn to show piety at home and to repay their parents. . . . But if anyone does not provide for his own, and especially for those of his household, he has denied the faith and is worse than an unbeliever" (1 Timothy 5:4, 8 NKJV). That shouldn't be interpreted as saying the whole burden needs to fall to one person—only that seeing proper care is provided is our responsibility.

The National Family Caregivers Association has a document called "Defining the Help You Need." In it they write, "Despite the fact that family caregivers are drowning in responsibility, they often respond 'no thanks' when help is offered. Asking for and accepting help is a complex issue. Obviously you first need to admit that having some help will make a real difference in your loved one's quality of life, and therefore yours as well. Then you need to define what help you need." Their suggestion is to ask:

* Which tasks or chores would be the easiest to ask others to do?
* Which do you really want to do yourself?
* Which, if any, can you afford to pay others to do?[29]

Levels (and Costs) of Care

In the opening story we get a picture of one kind of hands-on help a paid caregiver can offer. The Visiting Angels website describes care similar to what Jennie provides as: "Companion care and personal care services . . . these may include fall prevention, medication and fluids reminders, light housekeeping, grooming or bathing assistance and running errands" (www.visitingangels.com). In these categories, services are offered for a fee, some of which may be subsidized by a state or local agency. According to Genworth Financial's *2007 Cost of Care Survey*, this level of service from a licensed provider averages $17.46 per hour across the U.S., although local rates may vary from that average.

But there are other categories of care, as well.

At the lowest level many communities offer telephone reassurance checks. This may be a free service. In Chicago, for example, seniors who live alone can register with the city to receive free check-in calls. In subzero temperatures the city will call to be sure the senior's heat is functioning; in extreme heat waves, they'll call to be sure the senior is cool—or see that he is taken to a cooling center.

Close to this category of care are meal services such as Meals on Wheels and transportation services that give seniors rides to grocery stores, shopping centers, senior centers, or medical appointments. These are low-cost or free services available through many communities. Where we live, I often see handicap-accessible buses picking up and delivering seniors. Our city offers discounted taxi service for seniors. My grandmother carried a program ID card, and she could have a taxi pick her up and take her to a restaurant, grocery store, or even her beauty shop—wherever she wanted to go—granting her independence although she'd chosen to give up driving.

Then there is another category—again with a range of services and costs—that provides in-home medical assistance. These vary in rate depending on whether or not the care provider is Medicare certified or simply licensed. The average cost for Medicare-certified providers in 2007 was $32.37 per hour; for noncertified but licensed providers it was $18.57, according to Genworth.

Marlee's dad had advanced Parkinson's disease and later suffered a stroke. She and her mother determined that even with the family pitching in, they needed trained assistance. Marlee recalls,

We hired a woman who came five days a week for "wake-up and tuck-in service." She got Dad up, helped him eat, shower, dress, and get ready for the day. Then she came at night to do the reverse, get him settled in and changed and ready for bed. It was an expensive service, but so helpful.

On Saturdays when the caregiver didn't come, I would

shower him; on Sundays my brother would take his turn. But we work and couldn't be there during the week to do it for Dad. These services made it possible for us to keep him at home and for us to keep our jobs.

Services like these are more necessary now that hospital stays are getting shorter. Critical care nurse Jeanette says, "The hospital is full of sick people. The quicker you can safely get home, the better you are. In fact, the definition of 'safe to go home' has changed. You may still have tubes or IVs. I am amazed at how quickly patients' families can adapt to taking care of these."

She says this is one time no family should feel reticent about obtaining help from a health-care provider: "A visiting medical professional can show you what to do and follow up on the care—assessing how you're doing with it."

Often these post-hospitalization services are covered by Medicare or the patient's health insurance. When my dad came home after heart surgery and a stint in rehab, his insurance provided a visiting nurse several times a week to check incisions, do physical therapy, draw blood, and report vital signs to his doctor.

Where to Look

The answer to the question of where to find this kind of care varies by state and locale. Marlee looked in her local Yellow Pages under "home care" to find organizations called Helping Hand and Home Helpers—who employed the women who provided "wake-up and tuck-in" service. Similarly, organizations like the one that employs Jennie are nationwide and have websites.

Senior centers and state agencies on aging also offer referrals. And churches may be a great resource—one we'll discuss in the next chapter.

Often, however, the best resources are found by asking other family caregivers and medical professionals. Dad's visiting nurse came through the hospital where he'd had surgery. Barbara found her mother's live-in companion through a referral from the rehab center. And my mom and I had asked Jennie to take on my grandma as a client—only Grandma died before Jennie could begin her visits.

Caring Caregivers

Perhaps one more word from Jennie can help us feel more comfortable with sharing the burden, because her heart for the people she serves is one of Christlike compassion and tender, loving care.

One lady I visit in her home is on a walker. Yet I take her shopping with me for her groceries. Usually she will stand in one location, and I'll go around the store and get everything she needs; then she'll walk to the cashier with me. She is slow. But I'm patient. This is her one outing every week. What else does she have? How could I leave her home while I do her shopping for her?

That thoughtfulness is why Mom and I asked Jennie to partner with us in Grandma's care. She is exactly the kind of helper we'd want to entrust with our loved one's well-being.

Closing Prayer

God, I'm beginning to see that in trying to see to my parents' care all alone, I'm doing them and myself a disservice. I ask that You make me willing to ask for help from friends and family and even outside agencies. Please help me locate the right helpers to come alongside me in this journey.

Take *Action*

1. Take the National Family Caregiver's Association three-question assessment of the kind of help you'd find useful.

2. Discuss your challenges with family members.

3. Talk with your parent's medical team about caregivers with a proven track record.

4. Check with a senior center or your state's department on aging to learn about services and government subsidies.

5. Check these websites for help in locating caregiving help: Eldercare Locator: www.eldercare.gov or National Respite Locator Service: www.respitelocator.org.

Chapter Fourteen

HARD OF HEARING
and Hard of Listening

Gentle correction when

adult child knows best

Marcy Knows Best

My *mom was widowed at thirty-six. She was used to doing everything for all of us, and of course for herself. So it was hard watching the gradual role reversal, shifting toward us caring for her. We wanted to keep her safe. But being put in a position where people—even people she loved—were constantly checking on her was humbling. No matter how hard we worked to keep it from happening, she felt condescended to, belittled.*

Cooking and entertaining were Mom's favorite things. She was in her element when she was treating people—even us—like guests in her home. As dementia took over, she would bake the same things every day, but each time she'd leave out key ingredients. Then three years before she died, we began coming into her apartment in our home and finding the gas left on. Or we would smell smoke from things she'd burned because she forgot about them in the oven. Her cooking became a danger—to her, to our children, to our home. We had to turn off the gas to the stove.

She kept asking, "Why isn't the stove working?" We'd tell her it was broken. I can't tell you how many times this exchange went on. Eventually, we couldn't even leave a toaster in her kitchen—because she'd try to jam things into it and it, too, became a fire hazard.

She also had nighttime fears associated with her dementia. She would barricade herself in her apartment. Instead of keeping her safe, this kept us from being able to get in to help her when she would fall. Because she refused to use nightlights, her apartment would be pitch-black when she'd roam restlessly in the night. We had to take the lock off the door so we could get to her in an emergency.

OF ALL THE CHALLENGES in caring for our parents as they age, perhaps the most emotionally intense is the one when suddenly father doesn't know best. When his judgment is impaired by illness, like dementia, or by an inaccurate assessment of his own limitations, we adult children may be tempted to seize the reins of control and strong-arm our decisions upon him. This sets us up for an adversarial relationship and a heap of trouble.

Three pesky issues tend to take on astronomical proportions in this power transfer between parent and child—the right to drive a car, the right to cook for herself (or make his own food choices), and the issue of taking medications. We faced all these with Gram.

Gram drove until she was eighty-five. In our state, she had to take a behind-the-wheel driving test with a DMV instructor once a year—and each year she passed. She chose to limit her driving to a three-mile radius of her condo. Between DMV tests, Mom or I would ride with Gram periodically, to be sure she was still able to handle traffic challenges.

Just before her eighty-sixth birthday, she told us she didn't want to drive anymore. We were delighted she made this choice—as we had been feeling iffy about her reflexes and were discussing how we would take her car away.

With the cooking issue, we had more trouble. We'd bring hot meals from our kitchen, and she'd freeze them—we found servings of our food in her freezer after she died. We'd bring food from her favorite restaurant, and it would find its way into the garbage.

A year before she died, Gram began having trouble using her stove. She claimed it wouldn't shut off, so we brought in a repairman. He found it worked perfectly, but when he asked her to show him what she thought was wrong, she couldn't remember how to turn it on—let alone off.

Being a savvy adult child himself, he gave Mom and me a wink and began telling Gram a story about how much it would cost—$500—to replace the circuit board. *She* decided not to replace it and considered the stove "broken." She contentedly switched to her toaster oven, saving on forearm burns, fire hazards, and hysterical calls to us when she couldn't get the oven to turn off (the toaster oven shuts itself off).

They're Still Our Parents

Those exchanges were easy in comparison to getting Gram to take her medicine. She refused to take her prescribed water pills, opting to do holistic self-medicating by eating foods with high diuretic qualities. No cajoling from her doctor or counsel from our pharmacist could change her mind.

One day when we tried to force Gram to take her meds, she took her cane and swung it at Mom and me. (Yes, we're quick to duck.) She was that angry, that determined, and that frustrated.

At that point Mom and I decided to choose our battles. We can't win every war; sometimes we need to retreat. We decided to give up that no-win fight, and Gram lived five happy years without those meds and the side effects she attributed to them.

It's not unusual to reach these impasses, according to author Virginia Morris: "You should be sure your parent's bills are paid to protect him from utility cutoffs and eviction. You have to disconnect the gas to the stove if your mother, in her distracted state, is at risk of burning the house down. You must stop her from driving if she is a hazard to herself and others. You may need to find some way to get her to take her medications if she is forgetting them. But beyond these issues of dire risk and mental incompetence, your duty to protect your parent is superseded by his right to make his own decisions."[30]

We may be tempted to feel as if we are now responsible to *parent* our parents. But that's a patronizing attitude that only makes matters worse, according to Morris. "Your parent is and always will be your parent, and you will always be her child." She writes, "Are you the parent now? The answer is a flat-out and very definite NO. You are not parenting your parent."[31]

Where Morris is vehement, elder-care physician Dr. Thomas Cornwell doesn't hesitate to call this state of affairs "parenting your parent"; or he uses the picturesque term "geriatric un-development." He says when dealing with housing, financial, legal, and particularly health-care decisions with parents in a state of geriatric un-development, the "goal is to end all discussions peacefully and not to seek victory" while working toward a parent's best interests. He counsels, "Start with what you have in common: start with love."

Listening: The Ultimate Respect

I like that bit of counsel: start with love. Loving concern from a tender heart won't be bossy, controlling, domineering, or condescending. I keep going back to the scriptural command we've mentioned several times: "Honor [give weight to] your father and mother." Give weight to their best interests. Give weight to their desires. Give weight to their value as adults with life experience. Give weight to what's important to them.

One element that strikes me as helpful is that we can't know what's important to them, what's hurting or confusing them, if we don't genuinely hear what they have to say.

I tease my dad about the fact that his hearing isn't all that great and his *listening* is even less attuned. We joke about it, but it's all true—as is one other fact I'd rather not admit: I may need a listening tune-up myself. When it comes to what he wants, I am tempted to be as hard-of-listening to him as he is to me. While I may be hearing his words, am I taking the time to look in his eyes to try to discern his deeper meaning?

A pivotal component of successful communication is paying attention to words and nonverbal cues. When I wrote *Staying True in a World of Lies*, I included this story from cardiac care nurse Rene:

> I had a patient who had a complication after heart surgery. It was a minor complication, but it delayed his discharge from the hospital by several days. He kept complaining and asking why this had to happen to him. I could see an anxiety and a need just by looking at his eyes.
>
> So, I said to him, "What I'm sensing is that you are anxious to get home. Is there something pressing in your life that you needed to be home to finish?" He said yes. So I followed up by asking, "Is there a friend who can help you get done what you need to get done by the deadline?"
>
> He said, "Yes. Maybe I should make that phone call." He made the phone call, got his business taken care of, and we never heard another complaint from him.[32]

We often hear one thing spoken, but it's hiding another issue of greater concern to our parents. Only careful listening can lead us to the heart of the matter. So, in giving weight to our parents—out of respect for them and our Lord Jesus—our first step is truly listening.

Cooperation over Compulsion

Our second step is eliciting cooperation rather than issuing edicts. The website www.strengthforcaring.com includes this reminder:

"Keep in mind that you are still communicating with an adult. And most adults like to be asked to do something, rather than told what to do. As such, utilize the three magic words: 'can,' 'will' and 'please.' 'Can you stand up so I can fix your dress?' 'Will you sit in this chair?' 'Please join me in the living room.'"[33] This may be why author Morris cautions us against thinking of ourselves as parents to our parents.

Elder-care expert Carolyn Anderson confirms this counsel, "When talking with your aging parents, it's important to use an approach that lets Mom or Dad know that you want to understand him or her better and that you are not trying to take over his or her life. Your approach should show a willingness to work together."[34]

Anderson includes these active suggestions for eliciting cooperation:

* **Provide** information to your parents regarding options and decisions that affect their lives.
* **Include** your parents in the decision-making process.
* **Ask** questions—don't assume that you always know what your parents need or what they want.

The "P" Word: *Patience*

Anderson also offers this tidbit that makes me bristle: "If you find your parents uncooperative, listen and be patient." Now, there's a lesson I've hated learning. I don't think I'm alone. Laura fessed up to the same feelings about getting her uncooperative mother-in-law settled into an assisted-living facility: "I have to watch my own attitude. I'm not good with the elderly; I'm impatient. The Lord has convicted me of this."

Patience, according to *Strong's Concordance*, comes from a Greek word that means "cheerful or hopeful endurance, constancy." The usage is dotted throughout the New Testament—and attributed as a character trait of God. "Now may the God of patience and comfort grant you to be like-minded toward one another" (Romans 15:5 NKJV). Translation: God is patient; now, be patient with each other.

And Paul adds this prayer, "Now may the Lord direct your hearts into the love of God and into the patience of Christ" (2 Thessalonians 3:5 NKJV). The prayer gives me hope. Because the initial command to be patient (especially in the caregiving role) may not be one I can fulfill on my own, I appreciate the fact that someone out there—perhaps Christ Himself—is praying I'll exhibit patience. In His strength, anything is possible.

Protecting Them from Themselves

But sometimes all these efforts aren't enough. Sometimes for their safety, we need to be the "bad guys" and insist on protecting our parents from themselves. For example, in the question of whether or not your parent should be driving, here is a list of five warning signs of unsafe driving prepared by Kay Nelson, who manages a Helpline/Safe Return chapter:

* Forgetting how to locate familiar places
* Failing to observe traffic signals
* [Becoming] easily angry and confused while driving
* [Using a] speed not right for conditions
* [Exhibiting] poor judgment of distance (turns that are too wide or too tight, running over curbs)[35]

Experts suggest when we see the need to limit or curb our parent's driving, we proceed cautiously but firmly. Perhaps we can get a trusted person (like a doctor or insurance agent) to advise our parent against driving. That's what Isabelle's sister did:

My brother was behind Mom as she was driving home from

church one night. She pulled off the side road onto a main highway, and she drove the short distance home on the wrong side of the road. My brother watched in horror as cars were running off the side of the road to miss her. He pulled into her yard and asked her about the incident. She told him that was not so. Why would he say that about her?

It took some time, but eventually Isabelle's sister got their mother's doctor to convince her to quit driving. Since many elders have respect for authority figures like doctors, the counsel to give up car keys may be better taken from them than an adult child.

Giving Them Space When We Can

Nearly every expert agrees that the issue of losing their independence—especially to the children they once reared—is not easy. In chapter 3 Dr. Jennifer Thomas noted lost independence can lead to sadness and depression. "It can be difficult if they feel they've been put out to pasture," she says.

I don't know any of us who want a parent to feel that way—no matter the specifics of our relationship. But in taking to heart the counsel of choosing our battles, becoming active listeners, cooperating rather than dictating, and living out patient love like Christ's, we can reassure our parents that even when we disagree on methods, we share a common love and want God's best for them.

Closing **Prayer**

God, I ask You to give me a clear picture of any places my parent is becoming a danger to himself or others. Give me the courage to make those situations safer for everyone. Equip me to act patiently and lovingly—in Your strength.

Take *Action*

1. If your parent is still driving, ride with him periodically. If you see areas of concern, enlist a professional (or even a driving instructor) to assess his driving.

2. Make your attitude—of loving patience and compassion for your parent's loss of independence—a matter of prayer this week.

3. Block out time to listen to what your parent has to say about any situations where you may disagree. Pay attention to nonverbal cues. Be willing to elicit your parent's cooperation rather than insisting on your way.

Chapter Fifteen

LONG WALK
off a Short Pier

Caring for the caregiver,

before it becomes an emergency

Olivia's Confession

I am exhausted.

Medical appointments. Surgeries. Decisions. Papers. Administration. Bills. Scheduling. Bank statements. Medications. All on top of a full work schedule and trying to maintain relationships with my four daughters and five grandchildren.

Initially when my mom moved in, my brothers assumed I would take care of everything. They would be available if I needed anything. When I didn't ask, they assumed everything was okay. I found myself resenting that. I was getting exhausted with the details of taking care of her. It was more than I had anticipated. I had to give up my social life. I cut back on involvement at church. I was getting run-down with no place to go and get filled back up again.

I was being kind of a martyr—thinking I had to do it all without any help. But at the time I saw it as my responsibility alone.

I finally came to the point where I either needed to ask for help or drop. I struggled with letting my brothers know. But asking for their help was easier than I realized. I started by having a straightforward talk with them. They were willing. They did respond. And now we have a stronger understanding and good communication—and I have much-needed help.

I also turn to the Scriptures for strength. I love Philippians 2, where Jesus is described as a servant, surrendering to the Father. The attitude He had in serving blows my mind. That is my example. Whether serving Mom or someone else, I need to do it all surrendered to the Lord and serving with a happy heart, being gracious and kind.

I think, too, of Galatians 5:22–23, the fruit of the Spirit. I get drained and tired and irritable—and that will come out of my mouth. But these verses equip me. Up or down or hard or easy or convenient—I want to be consistent in demonstrating the attributes of God.

I made a commitment to take care of my mom. I didn't know how long or how hard it would get. But I made the commitment to my Father in heaven to take care of her. I realize I am serving Him in doing that— and it makes me want to do it well.

CHRISTIAN PSYCHOLOGIST Jennifer Thomas makes a statement that fits well as we open our discussion on watching out for our physical, emotional, and spiritual health. Her word picture has to do with a familiar scene to those who travel often. We board an aircraft, stow our belongings, and open our laptops. The flight attendant asks for our attention, but no one looks up. Still, she prattles on about emergency exits and lighted aisles, and ends with a statement about oxygen masks dropping from the ceiling. If they do, she instructs us to "secure your mask first, before helping others around you secure theirs."

Jennifer applies this counsel to caregiving: "You can't help your mom or dad if you have passed out yourself. Secure your mask first. Caregivers need to take a break." That's easier said than done for many who, like Olivia, have the mistaken idea that all responsibility falls on our shoulders.

Take flight attendant Marie—who has given the oxygen-mask spiel to inattentive passengers thousands of times. Even though she has three siblings who are willing, available caregivers for their dad, Marie says she fights feelings of, "If it's not me, it's not done right." She admits her over-involvement in her dad's welfare recently prompted the family doctor to caution her to "'back off before you become ill yourself.' He told me, 'Get a life!'"

While the wisdom of that counsel is indisputable, it's difficult to apply. She feels guilty taking a few hours for herself, even after working long international flights. "Today, I had to unpack and go through mail after a trip. Dad told me I didn't need to come over. As hard as it was to back away, I took that time for myself. And it all turned out fine."

Mixed Up and Ready to Crack

We're tempted to brush the issue of caring for the caregiver under the rug, paste on a smile, and never admit we have divergent feelings about caring for our loved ones.

Yes, there is the privilege—giving back to those who gave to us. But on endless weeks that string together into months and years of exhaustion and isolation, the feelings aren't nearly so lofty. They're closer to wishing we could pull covers over our heads and escape into the fantasy that caring for those in our chaotic orbit is someone else's duty.

The common denominator for nearly every caregiver is the feeling, at one time or another, of being mixed up, overwhelmed, and ready to crack.

Frances cared for her dying mother in her home. Later she was making decisions pertaining to her father's affairs when he died after what was to be a routine surgery. At one point during her father's illness, Frances arrived at her office only to get a strange look from her longtime employer. She recalls, "I was drained when I came to work.

My boss took one look at me and said, 'Just go!'" Following her boss's gaze, Frances looked at her feet and realized she had two different colors of shoes on. "That's how mixed up I was," she says. "They weren't even the same kind of shoe." It's funny now, but at that moment, it made her want to burst into tears.

While emergency situations may mean we temporarily neglect our appearance or well-being, we can't maintain an overwhelmed, overcommitted mind-set indefinitely without paying with our health. A *Quality of Life* booklet passed to me by our life insurance agent contains these facts:

> Caregivers become isolated and lose touch with social contacts, which can worsen stress and have a negative impact on overall health. . . . Many caregivers report significant personal health problems, ranging from minor complaints to serious, chronic disorders. A few studies have suggested that some caregivers may experience stress-induced health changes that may increase the risk of heart disease or cancer in susceptible individuals. A series of studies have linked the chronic stress of caregiving with impaired immune-system function, which makes the caregiver more susceptible to infectious conditions such as flus or colds, and may slow healing processes after an injury.[36]

The connection between stressed-out caregivers and these serious medical conditions ought to cause us to take notice.

Short-circuiting the Guilt

There is no sin in feeling overwhelmed, no matter that our innate feelings of guilt may try to convince us otherwise.

As I write, we've just turned the calendar to a new year that Mom and I are praying will be less stressful than the one we've just lived through. We're both entering this year exhausted, short-tempered, and frustrated. And, yes, guilty about those swirling feelings.

Finally, three days before Christmas, we wrote our annual Christmas newsletter. As we crammed onto one page a partial chronicle of the year's events—Dad's many illnesses, Gram's illness and death, number of ambulance rides, days spent in medical waiting rooms, number of funeral messages given—we made a startling realization: we have every right to feel overwhelmed, grieved, fatigued, and all those nasty emotions we were trying to ignore. These are byproducts of the year we've endured.

Not to allow ourselves an opportunity to work through them would be unhealthy. We now realize we need time to just "be," even though at the opening of this year we still have at least as many responsibilities as we had this time last year.

Experts say these conflicting emotions are natural. According to Barry Jacobs, Psy.D., a clinical psychologist and author of *The Emotional Survival Guide for Caregivers,*

> Family caregivers commonly experience a range of emotions that include shock, sadness, worry, anger, dread, guilt, loneliness, pride and gratitude. These are all human responses to challenging circumstances. . . . Sometimes caregivers can deal directly with the emotion and allow themselves to feel it while other[s] busy themselves as a way to avoid the feelings. In my opinion, caregivers are healthier and provide better care to their loved one when they . . . reflect upon what they are feeling.[37]

Making a Move toward Self-care

On Johnson & Johnson's caregiver website "Strength for Caring," I found practical, commonsense ideas that became the framework for my New Year's resolutions. I'll share them with you, in case you need to do something nice for yourself.

[Caregiving] can be a day-in, day-out grind . . . without a day off. As the days fill up, it's important to remember to schedule some time for yourself, as impossible as that may seem. Here are some simple steps you can take to recharge:

* Call a friend
* Go for a long walk
* Curl up with a book
* Rent a favorite video
* Take a hot bath
* Have a massage
* Write a letter
* Listen to your favorite music
* Take 10 minutes to do whatever you like best[38]

After reading this list, I popped in my favorite movie (*The Philadelphia Story* with Katharine Hepburn) and ripped four hours of music from my CD collection to compile a favorites list that's playing on my computer as I work.

Is it helping me feel refreshed? I won't be winning any Miss Congeniality competitions, but I am emotionally able to tackle today's responsibilities with focus, which is an improvement.

Support and Support Groups

These are simple, quick fixes. But they don't get to the heart of the problem, which may be either overcommitment—trying to jam too much into limited hours—or the inability to process the emotions of watching a parent decline.

For the overcommitted caregiver, sources of respite care and opportunities to outsource daily tasks like grocery shopping, cooking, and housekeeping can help free the caregiver to do those things only she can do, as we discussed in chapter 13. Jennifer Thomas says these services help by "setting margins in other areas to compensate for areas where caregiving encroaches on margins."

Additionally, in 2006 President George W. Bush signed the Lifespan Respite Care Act, to make it easier for American caregiving families to obtain respite care. The law provided $289 million in grants to states for developing respite programs. According to a report on the act in *CAREgiver* magazine, "Respite . . . provides caregivers with occasional relief necessary to sustain their own health or attend to other family members."

For the caregiver who needs to talk out her emotions with an understanding listener—support groups and professional counselors are available to help us process it all. Jennifer Thomas suggests two sources for locating Christian psychologists: Focus on the Family (800-A-Family) or the American Association of Christian Counselors (www.aacc.net), both of which screen and recommend Christian counselors.

Our local hospital recently sent an invitation to join a "Tender Loving Caregivers" support program, a monthly support group for caregivers providing care for an older adult. The brochure noted that, "In addition to support groups, the Resource Center offers classes and seminars that are designed to help family members care for themselves as they are caring for someone else." All are free services. Many hospitals are doing the same.

The brochure's last line is the reassuring fact all of us need to internalize: "You don't have to care alone."

A New Agenda

When Olivia mentioned key Scriptures that helped in her quest toward self-care, I resonated with her search. The passages she mentioned would be worthy of contemplation. Perhaps her enthusiasm will lead some of us to turn to Philippians 2 and Galatians 5 for our motivation. But I'd like us to examine another passage: Luke 10:38–42.

> As Jesus and his disciples were on their way, he came to a village where a woman named Martha opened her home to him. She had a sister called Mary, who sat at the Lord's feet listening to what he said. But Martha was distracted by all the preparations that had to be made. She came to him and asked, "Lord, don't you care that my sister has left me to do the work by myself? Tell her to help me!" "Martha, Martha," the Lord answered, "you are worried and upset about many things, but only one thing is needed. Mary has chosen what is better, and it will not be taken away from her."

You've probably read this passage many times—and you may relate with Martha and feel pained at Jesus' rebuke. I'm not going to add to Martha's heap of guilt—because I'm of the opinion that Jesus was tenderhearted, not mean-spirited, when He corrected this godly lady. (I wrote a study on Martha in my book *Transformed Women in the Bible*.) I don't believe Jesus was reacting against her service; He accepted it willingly during His last days on earth.

Rather, I believe the key is in one word—*distracted*. Martha was having an attitude problem that was causing her frustration. I suspect in her quest for perfection in preparation—wanting to serve Jesus with excellence—she was worried about 101 details that didn't matter in the light of eternity. Jesus was graciously freeing Martha of those meaningless details so she could get to the good stuff—relationship *with* Him and graceful service *for* Him.

I suspect He would tell us the same today in our service to aging loved ones: Olivia, Olivia . . . Frances, Frances . . . Marie, Marie . . . Julie, Julie . . . Reader, Reader . . . you are worried and upset about many things. The *He Cares New Testament* offers this challenge: "No matter what is on your to-do list today, take time to sit at Jesus' feet and learn from Him. Read His Word and slow down long enough for Him to speak to your heart and renew your weary spirit."

I resonate with this truth, and I believe in it lies the most useful respite for the weary caregiver. In its comments on Matthew 11:28–30, the *He Cares New Testament* asks, "Are your arms weary from trying to hold up your loved one? Is your back breaking from the weight of medical bills piling up? Is your mind exhausted from trying to keep track of all the appointments and medications? Jesus has an exchange He'd like to make: your heavy burdens for His light one."

Let's read and contemplate that invitation from the mouth of Jesus as we close this chapter: "Come to me, all you who are weary and burdened, and I will give you rest. Take my yoke upon you and learn from me, for I am gentle and humble in heart, and you will find rest for your souls. For my yoke is easy and my burden is light."

Closing **Prayer**

God, it helps to hear from Your Son that You understand my weariness and my overburdened feeling. Help me take on Your easy yoke. Help me know which expectations come from You and which are from self-imposed guilt. Help me find strength and a measure of joy in this season of service. Amen.

Take *Action*

1. Contact your hospital or senior center to find support groups and respite services.

2. Meditate on the Scripture passages mentioned (Philippians 2, Galatians 5, Luke 10, Matthew 11), and ask God to show you how to apply these.

3. Find a biblically based support group in your area. One source is HopeKeepers: www.hopekeepers.org.

Chapter Sixteen

FAITH
of Our Fathers

Raising eternal issues

with our parents

Julie's Uncle—Last-minute Confession

My Uncle Joey was one of the most colorful characters you could meet. He was actually my great-uncle, just a few years older than his eldest niece, my mother. I can still see him stirring a pot of spaghetti gravy (no, not sauce, our family calls it gravy) and meatballs on Sunday afternoons, serving up what he called a "spagnolia" party.

He and Aunt Marilyn lived a block from us. When I was in high school, Uncle Joey drove me to school, because it was on his way to work. I was a vocal evangelist during that era, and I often asked questions about where he stood with God. He'd deflect my questions and take another drag on his cigarette.

He'd heard the gospel countless times (when your brother-in-law is a pastor and your father is an evangelist, you will hear it). We couldn't count the times he'd heard he was a sinner in need of God's grace; but as far as anyone knew, he'd never responded.

When Alzheimer's sent him to a nursing home, Mom and I went to see him—hoping to catch him on a good day, when we could talk about Christ. It was a good day, but he remained in character, changing the subject every time we mentioned salvation.

Not long after, Aunt Marilyn called, telling us he'd been placed on hospice care. She asked if we'd come. As Mom and I raced to his bedside, we prayed for one more lucid moment—one more opportunity.

I knew he'd never have a long attention span, even on a good day, so at best I had a few phrases before his mind would wander. What would I say? This Scripture came to mind: "Everyone who calls on the name of the Lord shall be saved" (Romans 10:13). That's what I asked him to do: call on the name of Jesus. When I prayed a really short sinner's prayer, he squeezed my hand and moved his lips—although we couldn't discern his words.

Less than forty-eight hours later, Aunt Marilyn called to tell us Uncle Joey had died. But she also told us this story: As he lay gasping for breath, he'd looked up at her. She told him, "Joey, call on Jesus; say, 'Jesus, help me.'" With his last breath, he said, clearly, "Jesus, help me."

She asked me to give his funeral message, and I had the privilege of sharing this story to offer every family member present the assurance that "everyone who calls on the name of the Lord will be saved."

I WISH I COULD TELL you Uncle Joey's funeral was the last in my family for a long time. It isn't that I don't relish every opportunity to bring a gospel message to an audience. It's that I'd prefer to give a salvation invitation during a pleasant occasion—a baby shower or wedding reception. Yet I've given four funeral messages of hope to our extended family (for Gram and three of her brothers) in the last two years.

The situations were different between the brothers and their sister. Grandma was a pastor's wife. She came to faith in Jesus Christ as her Savior as a child in Sunday school. In her fleeting moments in ICU, she was able to call out to Jesus in the most natural way—as

Friend, Companion, Comforter, Prince of Peace. She knew Him personally, and when she called His name, she experienced the practiced assurance that He is, as the contemporary Christian songwriter put it, "as close as the mention of His name." Her funeral message was easy to prepare, all things being equal, because I could state with confidence that we don't "grieve like people who have no hope" (1 Thessalonians 4:13 NLT). I have no doubt Gram is enjoying heaven with her Lord this moment, even while Mom, Dad, and I are grieving her loss.

But Gram's brothers lived different lives. They, as she, had grown up in a godly home. But when they returned from service in WWII, they chose brides who didn't share the faith of their family; perhaps by default, they all chose to live away from their church. They loved their wives, their children, and each other. But no one knew the status of their faith. They weren't blatant in denying Christ, but neither were they vocal in confessing Him. Yet, before both of my other uncles died, their daughters called Mom and me to pray and read Scripture with their dads.

Witness without Words

I'd prayed about what I'd say; and I'd searched the Scriptures for the right words. But after the first two bedside conversations with my uncles, I wondered if I'd said enough—if I'd made it too easy. So I talked with my pastor, Colin Smith.

Not admitting that I was asking as much for my own assurance as for the book, I asked him, "How can an adult child bring up eternal issues with an aging loved one who isn't a believer? How hard should we push? How often should we bring it up?"

I stifled a gasp at Pastor Colin's initial response: "That's easy. Be quiet," he said, and paused for effect. What pastor would tell a parishioner to be silent about her faith, not to share her faith with a loved one on the brink of eternity? But rather than responding, *I* stayed quiet (no easy feat) and let him finish:

One Peter 3 comes to mind. The situation of a husband and wife—with the wife being saved and trying to convert the husband. The apostle Paul challenges her to be quiet, that he would be won over by the beauty of her life. The same applies to the situation you raise about a parent or aging loved one. The challenge is to be quiet and cautious about your words.

The problem here is that we need to be careful about the words we speak to a captive audience. It is easy for us to abuse the privilege in terms of evangelizing them in a way that is inappropriate and alienating.

Be careful in watching for the clear opportunity to speak, be sparing about that; avoid the snare of always speaking. And be sure we work on the beauty of our lives as believers. That will open the door for greater receptivity at the moment of speaking.

Aha. It sounds like another piece of biblical counsel: "Be quick to listen, slow to speak" (James 1:19). I thought back to the situation with Uncle Joey, captive in the car driving me to high school morning after morning, being peppered by my persistent (nagging?) questions. He turned a deaf ear, perhaps because they were mistimed words—and there were too many of them. I never waited for an opening to flow naturally out of conversation. I bulled right in. My motives might have been right, but I now see my methods were all wrong.

This conversation led me to think about the situation of Ruth and Naomi. There is no record in Scripture of Naomi giving her daughter-in-law a sermon on the inherently sinful nature of her soul—not to mention the heathen world where she grew up—or on her hopeless condition without a Savior. Instead, we have every reason to believe Naomi lived out her faith, even in her deepest grief, so convincingly that Ruth knew exactly what she was doing when she made that magnificent statement of faith: "Don't urge me to leave you or to turn back from you. Where you go I will go, and where you stay I will stay.

Your people will be my people *and your God my God"* (Ruth 1:16, emphasis mine).

What to Say, Given the Opportunity

Clearly, though, there comes a time when we must speak. At that moment what should we say? Again I turned to Pastor Colin. "Pastor, you know that often as people age, their attention spans are short due to pain or disease. Could you pare down the message of salvation to its leanest, clearest presentation?"

I don't know anyone who skillfully prepares a more insightful, biblically based message for his congregation week in and week out. We have to listen closely—even take notes—to get the most benefit from Pastor Colin's deep insights into the Word. So, when I asked the question, I was afraid I'd find I'd offered empty hope when I hadn't first taken the time to walk through the Four Spiritual Laws or the Romans Road with each uncle. Again Pastor Colin surprised me: "There is a one-word answer and a two-word answer. [Pause for effect.] The one-word answer is 'Christ.' The two-word answer is 'Trust Christ.'" His response bolstered my heart and reaffirmed the fact that I'd done the right thing in turning to Romans 10:13 for direction.

Then he illustrated with a story:

I'll tell you a story I heard yesterday. A guy was telling me that his father was in hospital—and not a believer. During the night a caregiver heard him call out something to the effect of "Holy Jesus! Holy Jesus!"

The nurse who heard it reported it to the son, saying, "I thought you might want to know."

By the time the son arrived the next day, the father couldn't communicate. But the son held his father's hand and told him what the nurse had said. "Were you trying to call on Jesus,

Dad?" he asked. "If you'd like to trust Jesus as your Savior, blink twice." And the father did. He blinked twice.

Openness to Eternal Things

According to psychologist Jennifer Thomas, the season of life our parents are living through most naturally brings up thoughts of spiritual things, even if they've never taken the time to consider their eternal destiny until now. "Often people have been busy leading their lives and not considering the question, 'What happens after I die?'" she says. "Then, they begin to lose significant people in their lives, and they ask, 'Am I ever going to see them again?'"

Dr. Thomas says this is a time when people of faith have a significant emotional advantage. "If they have faith in Christ, you know they aren't just going into the ground, but they are going into heaven." This gives peace even in grief. It illustrates the question I've asked many times, "What do people without Christ do in crisis?" They have no hope, but believers have "hope [that] does not disappoint" (Romans 5:5) because it's placed in the promises God offers through Jesus.

"There is a sadness to spiritual uncertainty," Dr. Thomas says. "Losing loved ones can be a distressing time if you don't have a sense that they are going to heaven." She says this is a time ripe with opportunities to use biblical truth to answer real-life quandaries of faith.

Samantha tells of the openness in these moments that can be found even in the most seasoned medical professional. When her father was dying, her family's longtime physician used to sit at her dad's hospital bedside just to hold his hand and chat with him after rounds were finished. Her dad never disclosed what they talked about—but he obviously had a great impact. Samantha and her sister Ava were shocked to see the doctor at their father's wake. Samantha teared up as she stood beside the doctor and looked down on her father's body. The doctor hugged her, and Samantha surprised herself by blurting out, "I am a Bible-believing Christian. I believe I will see my father again. This isn't the end of the line."

To which the doctor responded, "I believe that, too. My parents are both gone and I am confident this isn't the end of the line."

This memory of Samantha's brings to mind the passage written by the apostle Peter, "For our Lord Jesus Christ has shown me that I must soon leave this earthly life, so I will work hard to make sure you always remember these things after I am gone" (2 Peter 1:14–15 NLT). Her father's legacy was that his children and all those he touched would remember Christ's love long after he had passed into eternity. And that legacy cannot help but make an eternal difference.

Too Guilty to Be Saved?

It isn't unusual, when we're bringing up eternal issues with elder loved ones, to encounter their feelings of guilt over unresolved issues in the past—over wasted opportunities to confess or serve God. It's here that Jesus' parable (Matthew 20:1–16) of the vineyard workers can be a powerful tool. The gist is that the vineyard owner, a symbol or a type of God the Father, hires workers to harvest at several times throughout the day. Some work a full day; others work as few as one or two hours. When the owner pays the workers, he gives them all the same wage. This illustrates the fact that whether we've served Him throughout life or, like the thief on the cross, confessed Him with our dying breath, each one who calls on Him and trusts Him for salvation will be saved.

The devotional thought on this passage in the *He Cares New Testament* puts it in a helpful context:

> Sometimes people facing a health crisis think about turning to God but feel badly about doing so because they've pretty much ignored Him most of their lives. Their thoughts go something like this: . . . It doesn't seem right to go running to God now that I don't have much time left.

Yet, the parable shows us God wants us to come to Him—the earlier the better—but even the last to come will be with Him forever in paradise.

That's the message of love and open arms we can be ready to share with our aging loved ones—at that moment when God's Spirit opens the path for us to speak. In the meantime, let's take Pastor Colin's challenge to heart and live such beautiful lives before our loved ones even in our day-to-day, exhausting roles as caregivers, "so that, if any of them do not believe the word, they may be won over without words by [our] behavior" (1 Peter 3:1).

Closing **Prayer**

God, unless You prepare their hearts, my loved ones will never be able to understand the salvation I want desperately to share with them. It scares me that my everyday conduct can either help or hinder their journeys to You. Let them see only Jesus in my actions; equip me with more love and grace and compassion than is humanly explainable. Then, when it is time to speak, give me the words and the assurance that You want my loved ones with You in paradise more than I do. In Jesus' name. Amen.

Take *Action*

1. Become familiar with every Scripture passage you can find that explains salvation. Spend time in each passage, so it becomes a part of you.

2. Pray for God's supernatural ability to be a credit to Him in the routine tasks you take on for your parent.

3. Find believing friends who will pray daily for you to have an opening to share Christ's love (in actions or in words) with your parent.

4. Ask other believers to spend time with your parent, not to evangelize, but to be examples of Christlike compassion.

Chapter Seventeen

I GO TO
the Church

The family of God

supports caregivers

Karen Smith—Visits from the Pastor's Wife

I go to see Ted [pastor to senior adults at the church where Karen's husband Colin is senior pastor] once a month, and he gives me a list of people who need to be seen either because they are in hospital or they are lonely, have lost husbands, whatever. I go through the list and go back to Ted to get more.

My ministry is a bit different from others who do visitation, because people feel almost that they were visited by Colin. We have in our church a man who has cancer and has suffered a lot. I went to see him and his wife, and he said he felt part of the church in a new way and felt the church cared just because I went—which was a lovely thing to say.

There are several women in their nineties whom I visit regularly. One of them bakes me Swedish cookies and makes me tea whenever I come. She's just delightful.

I go to where they live and spend about an hour. I take my Bible and *have something prepared that I want to read to them. There is a beautiful prayer in the end of Ephesians 3 that I use often in my visits. Mainly, though, I read from the Psalms. Psalm 34 is one I use a lot. There are wonderful verses of comfort there. The Psalms are very human, aren't they?*

Then I ask them what they would like prayer for. We pray for that, and we pray through what I've read. When you're there praying for them, you're doing so much more than a non-Christian could because you can bring the comfort of the Scriptures.

Way back when we were in London, where Colin was pastoring, I went to visit a lady who'd had a stroke. She had lost her ability to talk. The only thing she could say was "No!" Sometimes the "no" meant "yes." It was difficult to tell. So, on my way to see her, I used to think, I need a whole list of things to talk to her about, because she can't talk back.

When I'd go into her room, she would always be there with her Bible open, and she'd be reading. So, I'd read to her all sorts of things. One day I thought, I'm going to read the Twenty-Third Psalm. Something familiar. Do you know that she said it all the way through with me? Just because it was right back there in her memory. It was engrained so deep. Isn't that amazing? And then later, I did the Lord's Prayer with her—and the same thing. She did that with me—every word, all the way through.

COLIN SMITH SAYS HIS WIFE is uniquely gifted with a sweet spirit that makes her a wonderful representative of Christ to the people she visits. One reason is that she genuinely cares. "When I go to visit, I write on little cards what they tell me—like the names of their kids—so I can remember. Then I write down what I read to them, so I don't read them the same thing again," Karen says. That extra touch may be one of the reasons those she visits feel so valued.

Yet, many of the caregivers whose stories you've read in this book are hesitant to ask the church for help. Some mistakenly believe there are others who need the church's resources more than they. Others don't know about helps their churches have in place. Still others may be too proud or too exhausted to ask.

Then there are those who struggle with aging parents who are—for lack of a better term—cocooning in a less-than-positive way. My grandmother spent her last five years not wanting to see anyone outside the family. Even *we* seemed an intrusion when we entered her domain. Although she'd been socially connected all her life, had even attended our new church with us after my grandfather passed away (you'll recall, Papa had been our pastor), now she didn't want help from anyone, least of all the church. When church ladies wanted to visit, she categorically declined their repeated offers—which placed a greater burden on Mom and me. Where we might have received respite, we didn't feel free to ask for or accept any.

Too often, then, the resources offered by churches go unclaimed—and caregivers continue to be overloaded. While we can't force loved ones to accept outside help, we can protect ourselves and our sanity by making good use of the support available to us through the body of Christ.

Perhaps the best place to start, as we begin to give ourselves permission to ask for help from our brothers and sisters in Christ, is with a question . . .

Why Should the Church Care?

That's probably a valid question, at least in part. Maybe not, why should the church care? quite so much a, why should the church use its staff and volunteer resources this way? After all, in the previous chapter we examined many ways the community at large offers trained assistance to our aging parents. So is it appropriate, necessary, or even profitable —from an eternal resources perspective—for the church to get involved? Pastor Colin offers a definitive response:

When we belong to the body of Christ, why would we trust our loved one to those who have no eternal connection? A care team [from the church] offers guidance, the ability to pray, a place to talk, even brings meals.

The church is a natural extension of family—relationships within the life of the church should reflect family in a healthy way. During last Sunday's sermon from Mark [3:33–35], I talked about Jesus saying, "Who is My mother and sister and brothers?" He points to the people listening and says, "Whoever does the will of My Father." Help ought to be extended through the family of God.

Essentially, he's restating a biblical concept: "Pure and undefiled religion before God and the Father is this: to visit orphans and widows in their trouble" (James 1:26 NKJV). The church has something to offer that the secular community can't—communion of a family with God as its Father.

Allowing others to come alongside us not only strengthens us for the journey, but gives our spiritual brothers and sisters opportunities to use their gifts. Listen to the way Jesus describes ministry to those in need. Perhaps you've heard this parable many times, but instead of seeing in Christ's description a destitute drunkard on skid row or a homeless child in need of shelter, picture your loved one as the one who was sick and visited by one of the King's servants.

Then the King will say to those on His right hand, "Come, you blessed of My Father, inherit the kingdom prepared for you from the foundation of the world: for I was hungry and you gave Me food; I was thirsty and you gave Me drink; I was a stranger and you took Me in; I was naked and you clothed Me; I was sick and you visited Me; I was in prison and you came to Me. . . . Inasmuch as you did it to one of the least of these My brethren, you did it to Me" (Matthew 25:34–36, 40 NKJV).

So, then, the complete answer to our question is that in inviting fellow believers to come alongside us in caregiving, we're offering them the opportunity to serve not just our loved ones, or even ourselves, but Christ. It's a win/win situation.

How Can the Church Provide Real Help?

Just as professional, paid caregivers provide services as needed, along a continuum of increasing benefit, so the church can help in ways large and small.

A monthly visit from someone on the church ministry team can be encouraging to homebound or lonely elders. We don't have to be married to the pastor to undertake a ministry like this one—we don't even need to be adults. Arlene Allen of the Assemblies of God points out, "Nursing-home ministry or shut-in ministry can be more of a blessing to the giver than to those to whom we go to visit. I used to take my young preschool son with me when going to the nursing home, because they loved to see small children. 'Can I hold him?' I was often asked. He was comfortable with the attention, and they always invited him to come back."

But perhaps more assistance would be welcomed. The church may have individuals ready to serve in tangible ways. I sang in a community choir last summer and talked with the pianist during intermission. She introduced me to an elderly lady in the audience. The lady took me aside and whispered in my ear this fact I'd never have guessed about the pianist: "She comes to my house every week and does my laundry. She takes me out to lunch while the clothes are in the dryer—and then comes home and carries them upstairs for me, because I can't get to the basement where the machines are." The elder lady isn't a believer, but the pianist is—and she sees herself as Christ's representative in this lady's life.

Many churches have a network of individuals trained to do these kinds of services. As Pastor Colin says, "Caregiving is not a job you can do on your own. One of the things the care team does awesomely is provide relief to caregivers." The care team at our church does hospital visitation and telephone follow-up, delivers home-cooked meals, helps with rehabilitation exercises, and more.

His church benefits from having a care team leader who is a retired critical care nurse. Because of her medical expertise, "there's an advice and counsel piece of the care team's work. They can offer caregivers someone to help them make informed choices when huge life decisions are being made. We benefit from having someone coordinating the team who is both a compassionate person and a trained nurse."

Stephen Ministries (Acts 6)

The ministries Pastor Colin and Arlene Allen describe are not isolated anomalies. According to the Stephen Ministries website, "more than 10,000 congregations from more than 150 congregations, in all fifty states, ten Canadian provinces, and twenty-one other countries" have been through that organization's formal training that equips "lay people to provide one-to-one Christian care to hurting people." The website claims, "More than 450,000 people have been trained as Stephen Ministers in their congregations."[39]

No matter their professional or educational backgrounds, these lay workers can offer services that allow care receivers to:

* Receive quality, Christ-centered, confidential care
* Know they are remembered and supported by their congregation
* Receive ongoing care for continuing needs long after the onset of a crisis, when many others have forgotten about them
* Grow in a deeper relationship with their Lord[40]

The ministry borrows its name from Christ-follower Stephen in Acts 6. Widows of the church needed care, so the disciples chose seven godly men, full of God's Spirit and wisdom (v. 3) to take responsibility for this crucial ministry. Stephen was among them. His calling was a ministry endorsed and prayed over by Christ's apostles. It was crucial to the care of the body—and to the testimony of the believers before a watching world.

Ways Churches Can Value Elders

Arlene Allen offers a list of suggestions on ways volunteers from the church can come alongside in caregiving. Her list is useful, because its goal is to help our parents feel valuable, useful, and constructive in God's kingdom:

* Telephone regularly.
* Read to them.
* Play a musical instrument.
* Sing to them and/or with them.
* Take them for a walk or wheelchair ride.
* Fix their hair.
* Reminisce about the "good old days."
* Make something for them.
* If they are shut-in, help them with cleaning or yard work.
* Write a letter for them.
* Send cards on special occasions.
* Give them a large-print calendar.
* Take them on short automobile trips. A trip to the cemetery where a loved one is buried would mean a lot.
* Take a small recorder to visit with an elderly individual, record the conversation, and later type it out.

A Caregiver's Respite

But the parent isn't the only one to benefit from this ministry. Karen Smith tells of an instance in a recent visit.

> I try to go when the family members are not going to be there—to space it out for them. The other day, though, I went to visit a lady who has kidney dialysis. This time her daughter was there. I had a wonderful chat with the daughter. But that's not why I went, really. I mean the mother did say the "odd thing" [translation: a few things here and there]. But the time when I'd gone previously, the daughter had been out, and then I had a more meaningful conversation with the mother.

As she relayed the story to me, Karen realized sometimes it is the caregiver who needs ministry—and perhaps that day, God knew the daughter needed the compassionate ear of the pastor's wife as much as—or more than—her mother.

Karen's memorable example of reading Scripture together with an ailing elder believer is a reminder of how powerful God's Word is in keeping aging parents connected with God's family. I spent a day of my personal devotions in Psalm 34 after Karen suggested that this is a powerful Psalm for those in the throes of aging issues. Several phrases from that prayer of David in distress made a meaningful connection in my heart. One that became special is verse 15: "The eyes of the Lord are on the righteous and his ears are attentive to their cry." There is no more comforting assurance than the fact that our God sees where we are and what we're facing; His ears are attuned to the heart cries we may not even be able to vocalize. Without a visit with someone from our church who truly cares, I might not have received that reminder on a day when I needed it.

Closing **Prayer**

God, sometimes I feel alone in caregiving. I want to honor my parents' wishes, but I feel the weight of my responsibility to meet their physical needs. Please, help me ask for help from my fellow worshipers. Show me how to ask and whom to ask. Then, please bless those who come alongside to offer me respite.

Take *Action*

1. If your church has a care team, talk to the coordinator about its services.

2. Spend a day of your devotions in Psalm 34, asking the Lord to provide you with His comfort and insight.

3. Confide in your pastor and/or his wife about your challenges and solicit their prayer support.

4. Seek others in your church who are caring for aging parents. Consider beginning a prayer chain or small group to support each other.

Chapter Eighteen

TAMING
the Grinch

Keeping both sides

of anger at bay

Melissa Looks Past a History of Abuse

As a child, I often wondered what I did to make my mother so angry
at me that she'd beat me, say cruel things, even throw things at me.
She'd leave me alone at home to do her housework, and come home to give
it a white glove test. I never did remember to dust the tiny crevices of the
dining room chairs—which always led to a beating when the white glove
came out.

She'd leave the cupboards and refrigerator empty. I'd scavenge
through her old purses for nickels and dimes, then take the bus alone to
the grocery store to buy food. She'd laugh and say I needed to lose weight,
which was why she didn't leave me any food.

I used to think my mother's tirades against me were normal. Then
I'd go to my friends' homes where mothers combed daughters' hair, cooked
their favorite meals, tucked them in at night, moved heaven and earth to
see that their lives were comfortable and happy. And I'd see just how
much I was missing.

When I grew up and married, I decided I'd never do to my family what Mom had done to me. And I never did. But her anger toward me never abated—except to become a little more Jekell and Hyde with the passing years. With others, she was sweet and darling. With my family and me, she was harsh and manipulative and downright mean.

Eventually she came to the point of needing my care. It was a spiritual and emotional struggle to be placed in the role of caregiver to the woman who had abused me. It was my husband who kept reminding me of God's command to honor her—to care for her to the best of my abilities. That always floored me, because she had been blatantly cruel to him all our married years—and he'd never done a thing to provoke her. Quite the opposite—he'd done everything he could to look out for her best interests.

My first inclination would have been to leave my aging mother to her own devices. That's what she earned. But it's not what would have pleased God. Somehow God (and the consistent love of my family) gave me the grace to meet Mom's physical needs—taking her to doctor's appointments, feeding her, chasing errands for her, seeing to her home repairs, maximizing her investments, whatever was called for.

But what I never had—and what I grieve for most now that she is gone—was an ability to let her all the way into my heart, where a mother should be. She died not really knowing me—or my family. Until the last moments of her life, whenever I'd let down my guard, even a little, she'd attack—with verbal or physical cruelty. Her anger was a danger to me. I had to protect myself from her, while seeing she wasn't left with an empty cupboard or scavenging for money to meet her expenses.

What I learned most through my season of caregiving was a lesson in the unmerited grace God has for me—the same grace He offered to me in relating to my mother.

EVER SINCE I TOOK PSYCH 101 as a college sophomore, anger has been an emotion that has perplexed me. Pop psychology says: Let it out. Spout it before it does damage to you. But God's way says: "Be slow to anger" (Proverbs 19:11 NKJV; also James 1:19); and tells us to "put off" this emotion that it groups with such despicable actions as malice, blasphemy, and filthy language (Colossians 3:8). Jesus calls unjustified anger a sin that endangers our eternal destiny (Matthew 5:22).

There seems to be a perplexing reality gap between the two approaches. That's one reason that broaching this topic—which rears its head on both sides of the caregiving equation—is not pleasant.

Another perplexing aspect is that it's not easy identifying anger's root, because it can spew out in situations that have little to do with its real cause. One adult son tells of his mother's explosion that began with his seemingly harmless observation that the telephone in her bedroom was smeared with peanut butter and jelly. Months later the family discovered that their mother's medical diagnosis of dementia was probably the source of this tirade and many other unprovoked episodes.

Finding Anger's Source

Despite a layman's difficulty in making a concrete diagnosis of anger's cause, there are a few sources that appear with some regularity in age-related situations: Much care-receiver anger is associated with approaching life's closing moments. Much caregiver anger is associated with overwhelming exhaustion. In identifying these wellsprings, we may be able to help diffuse anger and divert it into healthy expressions.

We'll begin by looking at anger's possible sources from our parents' perspectives.

Unfinished Business

The tragedy of Melissa's situation is that her mother died without apology, without amends, without resolution. Like many angry seniors, she left unfinished business. Consequently, in Melissa's heart lives an unresolved conflict that, if left unchecked, can leave her feeling bitter even though she'll never again be subject to new tirades of her mother's anger. Melissa will never know the true cause of her mother's rage—which likely had little to do with anything the young daughter did or said.

The guilt and pain of old hurts, their own abusive situations, and conflicted relationships can be a source of a parent's anger and be misdirected toward the nearest person—the family caregiver. Psychologist Jennifer Thomas is aware of this, and with her clients she does "an assessment of damaged relationships. I try to encourage them to see what they can do to go and be reconciled with people whenever possible, without harming themselves."

In her book *The Five Languages of Apology*, coauthored with bestselling author Dr. Gary Chapman, Thomas writes, "Few things are more powerful in human relationships than learning to accept responsibility for failures and to sincerely apologize to the person we have wronged."[41]

When a person is willing to resolve unfinished business, anger loses its grip and can be replaced with a loving relationship. Dr. Thomas tells of two brothers who hadn't spoken in fifteen years because of a bitter conflict over a mother's headstone. "One finally went to the other and said, 'I am coming back to tell you it doesn't matter. I just want to be your brother again.' The brother embraced him with open arms and wanted to make restitution." She observes that in reconnecting, they found joy and love in place of anger and disappointment.

Deterioration of Physical Abilities

We addressed a second source of anger in chapter 5, where we discussed querulous (cranky and difficult to please) parents. But it's worth a brief mention here, as it's a short step from querulous to angry. A parent's loss of self, of abilities she once had, of independence, of dexterity or health or strength can fester into anger that spews out at a caregiver.

Adult daughter Laura observes that the old myth that age mellows a person may not be true. She says she's seen in her mother's and mother-in-law's aging journeys that "aging magnifies a person's traits." If a person was sweet and compassionate in youth, she may mellow into a kinder, gentler person. But if she was bitter and fearful and angry in youth, she'll be that and more in her waning years.

Fear

Yet another source of anger is fear—in particular the fear of entering eternity. For those who have lived a lifetime without peace with God and the assurance of an eternity reserved in heaven for them (Colossians 1:5), death is a frightening prospect. It's a short hopscotch from fear to panic to venting anger.

Laura notes that even for believers, "Seniors have huge faith issues." These can include a feeling of isolation from God's family, of being trivialized or marginalized by the household of faith, or of cynicism as if God has abandoned them.

Consider Naomi from the book of Ruth. She had a huge faith issue in her elder years. She felt God had abandoned her—and she believed she was to blame, because she'd gone along with her husband's ill-fated plan to leave the Promised Land for the forbidden territory of Moab. In her fear and anger at the untenable losses she'd sustained, she gave some of the worst counsel imaginable to her two daughters-in-law: *Go back to your people and your gods.* Ouch. It was as if she was telling the young women, *You, who have come to faith, give up that faith because I'm living proof it doesn't work.*

What's an adult child to do with counsel like that—spoken out of fear and deep disappointment? Not what Orpah did—take it to heart and act on it. But rather what Ruth did—keep her own faith intact, speak and act in comforting ways, and stay the course side by side with the angry elder until the crisis averts and she sees the resolution in God's timing.

Medications and Illness

One more key source of anger in elders may be the one we caregivers are least likely to want to identify—illness. The son whose peanut-butter observation sparked a tirade was slow to recognize it. But illnesses like dementia, Parkinson's disease, and stroke can trigger anger, as can medications used to treat a variety of ailments common to seniors. Realizing a parent's anger may be a symptom of something he can't control can help insulate his family caregiver and keep her from taking it to heart.

A History of Abuse

But what of the parent who, in full control of her faculties, chooses to express abusive anger? In a case like Melissa's, what is an adult child to do? Pastor Colin says,

I want to speak sensitively to the person in this kind of situation. No one can prescribe what you must do for an abusive parent. The broad principle, though, is that the Holy Spirit of God is given to a Christian believer to enable us to move forward in the things God has spoken to us in the Ten Commandments.

What you would expect in a bad relationship would be bitterness, complete alienation, or even hatred. That is natural. But the Holy Spirit of God gives us something better than that. He enables us to overcome bitterness. In later life for an adult child to serve and minister to the very people who abused him or her—that can only be attributed to God's grace at work in the person of the Holy Spirit.

Counselor and author Jan Silvious would agree. In her book *Fool-proofing Your Life*, she tags those who are dangerous people in our lives *fools*. When they are our parents, she says that from the words of Matthew 15:3–6 (where Jesus discusses honoring our parents with our resources and our words) we can deduce,

> Being emotionally intimate, spending a lot of time together, and being "one big happy family" is not required if it is not authentic; but being kind and meeting needs are. As long as you can detach, forgive, and pray, you should be able to find the balance that God requires as you obey his command to honor your parents, no matter how foolish they may be.[42]

A Caregiver's Anger

Since we're turning our attention toward our choices and actions, let's look at our anger. Maybe your case isn't as extreme as Melissa's. But even in the best situation, one of the emotions we *will* experience while caregiving is bound to be anger. Anger as a function of grief. Anger as a function of exhaustion, as day and night commingle in one draining, endless work camp. Anger as a function of others who fail to pitch in to lighten our load. At times we will be gripped by anger.

So what are we to do with it? As it's not appropriate for the parent who can control his anger to vent it at his caregiver, so it isn't appropriate for a caregiver to mistreat her parent in anger. It's called elder abuse. It can happen to any of us if we stuff our anger day after day. That's when it explodes like Vesuvius in a cloud of molten ash.

"Be angry, and do not sin," the Scripture says. "Do not let the sun go down on your wrath. . . . And be kind to one another, tender-hearted, forgiving one another, just as God in Christ forgave you" (Ephesians 4:26, 32 NKJV).

The phrase about not letting the sun go down may be figurative, but its directive is certain—don't treat anger like a welcome guest in our hearts, pampering it, feeding it, giving it space and time to grow. Instead, express it appropriately—if possible as a calm "I" statement, as in "I don't feel the rest of the family is helping me in appropriate ways," or "I feel devalued when you speak to me that way."

If speaking calmly to the person is not an option, find a respite caregiver and sentence yourself to a time-out. Hospice worker Lois credits a visiting caregiver for giving her and her sister a break during their mother's deterioration. One trying day the worker came to them and told them to get out of the house. She prescribed a long walk to refresh their minds and bodies. Because they knew their mom was being well tended, this getaway revitalized them and diffused a tense situation.

Most of all, proper anger expression may mean being willing to forgive slights and another's words spoken out of frustration and fear. Jan Silvious says, "When you determine that another person's anger will not work on you anymore, all of the power is gone. You are saying, in effect, 'Rage on. You are not going to change how I feel about myself, about the Lord, or about you.' Once you take the power out of anger, anger will most likely go somewhere else."

This is consistent with the biblical principle: "A gentle answer deflects anger, but harsh words make tempers flare" (Proverbs 15:1 NLT).

An Understanding Heart

Dr. Alice Domar offers this useful prescription to caregivers who want to diffuse our parents' anger. Let's consider her words and then go to prayer:

It is difficult for a caregiver to truly understand what it is like to be the one who is aging and needs care. One of the most important skills you can develop as a caregiver is to listen. We must try to spend more time listening to our loved ones, rather than telling them what to do. Let your loved one make the decisions they can. Sometimes too much help can be no help at all, especially if it frustrates your loved one.[43]

Closing **Prayer**

God, I don't understand my own anger, let alone the anger my parent is experiencing. I ask for Your insight into how to help diffuse the anger in our caregiving situation and infuse it with Your grace and understanding. Help me listen—to him and to You— so I may act in ways always pleasing to You.

Take *Action*

1. Keep a log of times when your parent becomes agitated, and see whether there is a pattern that can give you a clue about anger's true source.

2. If abuse and anger are ongoing, seek a counselor or pastor who is equipped to help you process the emotions and find productive ways to express them.

3. Make a list of friends, church, and community services that can offer respite—and keep it handy.

4. Set emotional and, if necessary, physical boundaries so that, while being true to your responsibilities, you are not putting yourself or your parent in danger.

Chapter Nineteen

I'D RATHER
Be Blue

Combating depression

in parents and ourselves

Barbara's Mother Overcomes the Blues

After Mom's fall, she spent time getting stabilized in the hospital and getting her medications balanced. From there we had to check her into rehab. At the end of the thirty days of rehab allowed by Medicare, she hadn't made enough progress. She was horrified to learn we had to keep her in the nursing facility, because she wasn't able to go home.

It was a nice place—we'd looked hard (and paid plenty) to find a homey place. The staff treated her well. My sister and I visited often. But Mom was sad. She kept asking, "Why doesn't God heal me?" I kept answering, "God is sustaining you, Mom. We pray for healing and hope for it, but it is all up to God's will. For now, you have a little mission field here."

She wasn't convinced. She felt hopeless. She feared she'd never get home to play her piano. She was without purpose.

Mom used to love to crochet. So I got together all her crocheting gear *and lots of yarn and brought them to her. I suggested she crochet an afghan for my cousin's little girl. She agreed—but her lack of enthusiasm made me wonder whether she planned to follow through or she'd just said yes to appease me.*

At first, I'd go to visit her in the evenings and she wouldn't have touched the crocheting all day. I'd ask her about it—but she'd seldom answer. Then one day I noticed she was getting into it. Slowly the afghan was progressing—and with it, Mom was progressing.

I commented on how far it had come, and she replied, "I have to live long enough to get this afghan done." And you know what? She did it.

It wasn't long after the afghan was finished that we were able to bring her home. One Sunday a few weeks later, Mom and I went together to deliver the afghan.

I now realize the afghan was her purpose. It helped her stay focused and get well—it encouraged and motivated her.

THE LOW SPIRITS Barbara encountered—and combated—with her mom are as understandable as they are widespread among the elderly and their caregivers. In fact, according to the Dana Alliance for Brain Initiatives: "Studies suggest that at least one in four individuals who have a chronic illness also have depression." Dana Alliance's health and retirement study found that as many as 20 percent of men and women eighty or older exhibit "severe depressive symptoms"— a number only slightly higher than that for those in their seventies.

That doesn't take into account the larger number who, like Barbara's mom, are exhibiting the blues as a rational response to seemingly hopeless circumstances. Consider a few of the caregivers who have shared their stories so far:

* Melissa's mom's hunger strike was a symptom of the sadness and abandonment she felt as her inner circle of friends passed away. Special attention from loved ones and the healing passage of time drew her out.

* Marlee's mother, now contented in her senior-citizen apartment, was in the grips of sadness while she lived alone. No attention or love from her family ever seemed sufficient to draw her out of the blues.

* After her husband died, Ava's mother balked at attempts by her daughters to draw her out. She was the epitome of the old pop song "I'd Rather Be Blue." She demanded time to wallow. It went on long enough that Ava's sister Samantha contacted a Christian counseling center. But before the daughters could convince their mom to welcome help, they began to see signs that she was rejoining family life.

* Marcy's mother who suffered from dementia experienced sadness in her lucid moments because of her loss of "self"; while in her dementia she wept often, reliving losses of her husband, parents, and siblings.

* Dean's mother (from chapter 10) experiences a more dangerous variation of low spirits, as she has clinical depression and is dependent on medications to remain stable.

From these examples, we can begin to discern the range from the blues—which may be helped by caregiver attentiveness, purpose, and faith—and medically diagnosed depressive disorders that require treatment from a trained professional.

For those on the "blues" end of the continuum, families can be creative in drawing the parent out. Like Barbara did with the crocheting project, other suggestions might include, "Get them involved in different types of groups—social, church, exercise. Exercise, especially, gets the endorphins going and can decrease depression," according to Jennifer Thomas. "Aging parents often have lost their daily social support," and finding ways to reestablish a support system can decrease their inner sadness.

Then there's the other end of the continuum. According to the

Dana Alliance, "While it may seem natural to feel depressed and frustrated by persistent illness, depression is a serious medical condition that can be treated effectively in most people. . . . It is therefore important to consult with a doctor who has experience treating depression in the elderly, such as a geriatric psychiatrist."[44] So let's begin by learning to identify the issues that ought to lead us to call in expert help.

The Blues or Depression?

As with any medical condition, depression can be dangerous to self-diagnose. But understanding its key warning signs can be helpful if it leads us to know when to seek professional counsel—and let the pros do the diagnosing. The National Institute of Mental Health lists several key warning signs of depression:

* prolonged sadness or unexplained crying spells
* significant changes in appetite and sleep patterns
* irritability, anger, worry, agitation, anxiety, pessimism, indifference
* loss of energy and enthusiasm, persistent feelings of guilt, worthlessness, hopelessness, helplessness
* inability to concentrate or make decisions
* loss of enjoyment from once pleasurable activities
* withdrawal from social contacts, isolation
* unexplained aches and pains
* recurring thoughts of death or suicide
* memory loss[45]

Dr. Barry Jacobs, author of *The Emotional Survival Guide for Caregivers*, says if several of these symptoms "persist continually over a two-week period, it is wise to seek help from your doctor or a counselor." The October 2007 issue of *Mayo Clinic Health Solutions* newsletter is more aggressive in its advice: "If you have thoughts of harming yourself or others, seek medical help immediately."

This is wise counsel, according Dr. Thomas. But she cautions about too quick a diagnosis. When Dr. Thomas meets a client who is exhibiting these symptoms, the first thing she does is to rule out other causes. "I ask when they had their last blood test done," she says. "Because, for example, thyroid disorder can cause depression." In that instance, treating the underlying medical condition (thyroid disorder) supersedes treating the symptom. Only when medical conditions are ruled out is Dr. Thomas ready to "delve into detail with the symptoms."

Depression's Damage

Among those of older generations, when strong people didn't acknowledge emotional issues in polite company, seeking professional psychological help may seem a sign of weakness or carry with it a social stigma. Dr. Thomas says those who "didn't grow up with counseling" need to be reassured that "it isn't a failure on your part" to seek help.

It can be useful to remind a parent that depression is an illness that can damage the body. According to *Mayo Clinic Health Solutions*, here are a few body systems that can fold under depression's weight:

* In the **heart**, depression may be associated with abnormal heart rhythms, increased blood pressure, and faster blood clotting.
* In the **liver**, it can elevate cholesterol levels.
* In the **adrenal glands**, depression may result in chronically elevated levels of stress hormones.
* In the **pancreas**, it can elevate insulin levels.

✳ In the **brain**, depression can lead to unhealthy lifestyle choices, such as poor diet or lack of exercise.[46]

Just as the damage from diabetes or high blood pressure can be controlled by proper, timely medical attention, the same is true for depression—if properly diagnosed and treated.

Depression in Ourselves

Until now, we've been considering how to distinguish between persistent sadness and full-blown depression in our parents. But depression isn't age specific. The symptoms and dangers are the same for us as they are for our parents. The prescription is the same, as well. Dr. Jacobs points out,

It's not unusual for caregivers to occasionally feel sad. But there are important distinctions between sadness and depression. Sadness is an understandable and reasonable response to adversity or loss. Clinical depression is a psychiatric condition in which people feel a degree of sorrow and hopelessness that is out of proportion to the circumstances.[47]

He encourages caregivers to seek help for emotionally draining situations, whether we are exhibiting the symptoms of depression or experiencing sadness and exhaustion consistent with the weight of our caregiving responsibilities. He says, "The more you are attuned to [emotions], the better able you will be to care for yourself and then complete your mission to provide loving and quality care to your loved one."

Dr. Thomas's best counsel is to follow a parent's lead in seeking help, whenever possible. "Giving them a sense of control is crucial," she says. "Listening to them; drawing them out. Watching their behavior. If they are not functioning, get them to agree to see a counselor at least once. Life is difficult. Everyone could benefit from some counseling."

Seeking Help

Dr. Jacobs suggests seeking help from psychological professionals as one option. But he also recommends sharing feelings with trusted friends, pastoral counselors, and support groups.

Dr. Thomas agrees and offers this counsel for Christian believers who want to find counselors: "I recommend people find a match of faith and values with their counselor. A counselor influences her client's choices. You are more apt to feel comfortable with a counselor if you have that match."[48]

God's Presence Despite Depression

But perhaps we've done all we can to draw out a sad loved one, find help for a depressed loved one, and see to our own emotional needs. Even yet, one of the biggest questions we may continue to face is: "Where is God in all this?" It's the essence of Barbara's mother's "Why doesn't God heal me?" And it's the stumbling block nonbelievers often have to faith: "If God is good, why does He allow pain and suffering?"

I could quote platitudes about God working everything for good or understanding it all when we get to heaven. But spoken from a detached distance, these platitudes are unsatisfactory. The question still stands. Listen to how the weeping prophet Jeremiah asks and answers it in an emotive poem:

So I say, "My splendor is gone
      and all that I had hoped from the Lord."
I remember my affliction and my wandering,
      the bitterness and the gall.

I well remember them,
    and my soul is downcast within me.
Yet this I call to mind
    and therefore I have hope:
Because of the Lord's great love we are not consumed,
    for his compassions never fail.
They are new every morning;
    great is your faithfulness. (Lamentations 3:18–23)

Jeremiah has lost everything good from his past life, and he's downcast, filled with bitterness, overwhelmed by affliction. Sound familiar? Yet, he finds hope in the compassion of the Creator who "is near to all who call on Him" (Psalm 145:18) and binds the wounds of those who are brokenhearted (Psalm 147:3).

When Jesus came and changed the nature of our relationship with God—by inviting us past all boundaries and into His presence—still our question remained, because while those who have received God's forgiveness through Jesus' sacrifice aren't subject to eternal death, we're still earthbound in a place that is far from Eden. So the apostle Paul addressed the question in his writings to discouraged and downtrodden believers:

But if we hope for what we do not yet have, we wait for it patiently. In the same way, the Spirit helps us in our weakness. We do not know what we ought to pray for, but the Spirit himself intercedes for us with groans that words cannot express. And he who searches our hearts knows the mind of the Spirit, because the Spirit intercedes for the saints in accordance with God's will. And we know that in all things God works for the good of those who love him, who have been called according to his purpose. (Romans 8:25–28)

In both passages we find one pivotal word that makes up half of God's prescription for our down and depressed times: *hope.* All is not lost. There is hope because of the second half of God's prescription: Himself. He is present. He is faithful. He is loving. He is beside us and in our corner and at work above all we are seeing.

You're right if you've observed that at the end of Paul's passage we see the platitude I was tempted to rattle off earlier. Seen in context it loses its pat-answer status, though. The context is that we have hope, despite what we see, because God's Spirit is speaking to God the Father on our behalf—and He is at work *in* all the circumstances of our lives *to bring about* a good eventual result for those who love and serve Him. We may not see it now, but what we don't understand about how He is at work, we can entrust to the One who has our best interests at heart—ours and our loved ones.

Closing **Prayer**

God, depression frightens me. Sadness debilitates me. Yet these are interwoven with my circumstances. Please help me find the hope Your prophet described. Let me see a glimpse of how You are at work bringing about a good result from my difficulties. And help me find godly counsel to walk with me through this dark valley.

Take *Action*

1. Take the depression self-assessment at www.MayoClinic.com. Think of your symptoms first; then consider the questions in light of what you see in your parent.

2. Search the Bible for the word *hope*. You'll find it throughout the Psalms and in Paul's epistles. List all the characteristics of God that offer believers hope—and remind yourself of those often.

3. Use Dr. Thomas's criteria to locate a Christian counselor or support group for your parent and/or yourself.

Chapter Twenty

MEMORIES
Light the Corners

When forgetfulness turns serious—

the dreaded "a" word

(Alzheimer's)

Isabelle Sees Signs of Dementia—and Wants to Look Away

Mother was a high-energy person. I could see that she was aging by her white hair and wrinkles; however, I never viewed her as old.

Her mind left a little at a time over the course of eight years. It happened so slowly that I understand the phrase "the long good-bye." Maybe the gradual decline of her mind helped me emotionally, because I had time to adjust to every phase.

One day, I called to tell her I was coming for a visit. Mother acknowledged what I said and then told me that my niece's house had burned. She said the same thing again, and again. She didn't notice when I would try to insert something into the conversation. I called my sister and told her what happened; she told me the repeating was happening often.

We had never dealt with dementia, so we were clueless about what was happening. Maybe it was just what older people did.

The repeating also took place in her activities—Mother got up each morning, dressed, drove to the grocery store, and bought groceries. We wanted to respect her, so we didn't ask why. After a year of buying groceries every day, she had piled groceries all over—even in her bedroom. Eventually we told the grown grandchildren to go in the back door and "shop" for groceries in Mother's bedroom.

If she dozed off in her chair, she would get up and take a second dose of the same medicine she'd already taken that day. We had to hide her medicine. One of us would go over and give her the proper dose each day.

Some days she was sweet—she wanted to laugh and make up funny things. But the angry days were hardest to bear. I did lots of housecleaning those days—good therapy!

Before Mother's mind was really bad, I would read the Bible while I sat with her. It would trigger something in her mind, and she would want to read her Bible. One Sunday after church several family members ate lunch with Mother, and we got in a conversation about a religious topic. Mother began to speak her view, and it sounded so much like the Mother I remembered—but then the shades were drawn again.

Her last two months she forgot her name and had to be sedated so she wouldn't have violent outbursts. It broke my heart to see her act insane. I cried the last two times I saw her; Mother was gone before her body gave up the fight.

HERE'S A MEMORY-LOSS quiz for you: While you were at the grocery store together, your mom ran into someone she hadn't seen in a while and couldn't remember his name. Should you be concerned? At a family dinner last night your dad told the same story from his childhood that he's told eight hundred times over the years. Everyone at the table could have gotten to the punch line ahead of him—and all eyes (except his) were rolling in frustration. Should you fear the worst?

According to the Dana Alliance for Brain Initiatives,

Occasional forgetfulness is a perfectly normal part of life. Certain types of memory slips, such as forgetting names or where we parked the car, are common even among the young. In fact, in young and old alike, stress, sleep problems, certain prescription medicines, and depression are associated with memory difficulties. On the other hand, memory problems that significantly impair day-to-day functioning are cause for concern and should be evaluated by a qualified medical professional.[49]

Not every repeated story or forgotten acquaintance requires a doctor visit. But if we observe a pattern of forgetfulness that escalates to impair judgment and everyday function, this should motivate us to seek medical attention. Experts caution that some memory problems are irreversible, while others are treatable and reversible—if we get medical attention in time.

Dementia or Normal Aging?

Before we indulge our worst fears and form our own diagnoses, it would be helpful to understand that dementia is not limited to one cause. According to the National Institute on Aging,

> The term *dementia* describes a group of symptoms that are caused by changes in brain function. Dementia symptoms may include: asking the same questions repeatedly, becoming lost in familiar places, being unable to follow directions, getting disoriented about time, people, and places, and neglecting personal safety, hygiene, and nutrition.[50]

If we observe several of these symptoms, we'll want to talk with our parent about seeing his doctor. If he resists, we may need to make an appointment with his doctor to spell out our observations, so the doctor can be involved in creating an informed plan of action.

Once we've gotten our parent to the doctor, it is likely he'll ask extensive questions about our parent's medical history, prescription and over-the-counter medications taken, and history of brain injuries. He may order lab tests and high-tech scans (although Alzheimer's can only be diagnosed with certainty after death) and administer a test of memory, problem solving, counting, and language.

Once tests are complete, there is a range of possible diagnoses. Problems may be caused by reversible conditions like "high fever, de-hydration, vitamin deficiency and poor nutrition, bad reactions to medicines, problems with the thyroid gland, or a minor head injury." Or, they can be caused by a series of strokes called multi-infarct dementia. While the damage from these strokes is not reversible, it is a condition that requires treatment. Or, it can be caused by Alzheimer's, where "brain cells degenerate and the brain becomes littered with tell-tale debris, known as plaques and tangles."[51]

Decreasing Ability to Perform Normal Tasks

That's all clinical—maybe it sounds to you like medical mumbo-jumbo. But what does the early onset of dementia look like in daily life?

Best-case Scenario

While Alice's mom lived alone, she did have a caregiver who came in and set out her medication in daily doses—each dose labeled for each day. The problem arose when Mother couldn't remember what day it was—she never was quite sure whether or not she'd had that day's dose. While Alice decided to move her mom across country to an assisted-living facility near her home, the diagnosis of dementia's cause was twofold: her mom was depressed and lonely, and her medications were inducing the memory-loss symptoms. A move close to family and the proper adjustment of her medications caused the problem to clear up.

A Way around a Sticky Issue

Olivia's mother, a former grade-school teacher, exhibited memory loss in an inability to understand bank statements. She, too, was isolated and depressed—and frustrated over her inability to do what she'd always done. When her mom moved into Olivia's home, Olivia took over the checkbook, although her mom does have the ability to cash small checks. On the days when Olivia's daughter and grandchildren visit, Olivia notices an improvement in her mother. "They may take Mom out to Wal-Mart or to lunch—give her a break from the routine. With the two little ones, it is an *active* event. Those days when I come home, there is a marked difference in Mom's awareness level. She interacts with me and carries on a conversation."

Facing Facts Head-on

For Laura, who is supporting her husband as he makes caregiving decisions for his aging mother (diagnosed with dementia), the outcome wasn't as positive. As the daughter-in-law, Laura didn't have as much freedom to speak as she watched her mother-in-law deteriorate. Laura noticed that her mother-in-law's home in the city had fallen into disrepair. "One morning we found her just sitting on the basement steps." The visiting caregiver finally jarred the family into action, telling them it was time for Mom not to be on her own, so they found a semi-independent living facility. But when they moved her in, "she was making shrieking calls to us every day saying, 'I am forgotten!'" It took four months for Laura's mother-in-law to adjust.

Protecting a Parent from Harm

In all these stories, doctors and other outside caregivers were involved in helping families make informed decisions about protecting their parents from harm. Sometimes, as in Laura's situation, the professionals needed to bring the family face to face with reality.

What is obvious in these stories is that no family member can be the sole, full-time caregiver for a dementia patient. It would do a disservice to caregiver (an exhausted caregiver may become seriously ill) and care receiver (a fatigued, emotionally drained caregiver will be less patient and less attentive). In fact, caregiver depression is a frequent side effect of dementia care—and can be helped by sharing the load with friends, family, and trained professionals.

The resources for professional help are more plentiful today than ever. Government organizations like Eldercare Locator (www.eldercare.gov) can help locate and engage the services of part-time in-home help and even adult day-care centers. Doctors can provide referrals to social workers versed in available local resources. Churches may offer support groups, respite volunteers, and other services—as they fulfill their callings to "comfort all who mourn" (Isaiah 61:2) and support those whose faith is being tested, as if by fire (1 Peter 1:6–7).

A Faith That Works

Many times the last element of a parent's awareness to leave is her faith. Often old hymns soothe when nothing else will. Christian TV programs provide a few minutes of repose. Reading a Bible (or hearing it read) brings moments of peace.

Likewise, caregivers find in their faith strength that can't be explained away. The Scriptures are filled with characters like Job, David, and Paul—real people who struggled with grief and pain. God's promises to be "a very present help in trouble" (Psalm 46:1 NKJV) and His servant's affirmation that "You are my hiding place; you will protect me from trouble and surround me with songs of deliverance (Psalm 32:7) provide courage to go on when all human nature urges us to throw in the towel.

Laughter and Patience

Even for the caregiver who is trying to be Christlike in her role, it can be grueling to endure the incessant questions and endless repetition of dementia. Like Isabelle's mom, a parent may sound like a warped record—and any attempt to move the needle to another groove may feel pointless. Author Virginia Morris suggests an attitude adjustment may help: "You have to give yourself permission to laugh."[52]

Laughter helped Marcy's mother through her worst days. Marcy recalls, "My husband would tell the same jokes at dinner every night—which got old for the girls and me. But the jokes were new to Mom. Every time she'd laugh—and her attention would be averted away from whatever was irritating her."

Other opportunities for patience came when Marcy's mom would become agitated because a family member wouldn't come to visit. Having determined to be honest with her, Marcy or the girls would tell her that her parents or husband or sister had died. "It was horrible seeing her grieving over and over for the same losses," Marcy recalls. "The only good thing was that she'd forget about it as soon as her attention was diverted."

The family took a cue from this observation and used a different tactic. Granddaughter Holly (who has since studied to become a psychologist in a mental-health facility) recalls, "Rather than addressing her anger about that person not visiting, we would ask her what she remembered about him. That would get her telling stories—and she'd forget about his not visiting."

But patience isn't necessary only for the patient—it's something caregivers need to offer themselves. If we've been impatient with Mom for forgetting appointments, repeating herself, acting in quirky ways—we need to forgive ourselves for that. Once we know these actions are a result of a disease our parent couldn't help, it is natural for us to berate ourselves. But this is fruitless. We need to forgive ourselves and go on. Virginia Morris puts it well:

When your parent pours a whole bottle of shampoo on your rug because she saw a dirt spot, or throws dinner in the garbage because she saw bugs crawling on it (they were black pepper flakes), pause before responding. Just pause. Don't say anything. Look quietly at the situation and decide if it has truly ruined your life.[53]

A Difficult Story of Coping

Some things, though, are more serious than shampoo on the carpet or a ruined roast. Then, the most necessary skill for the caregiver is an ability to roll with the unexpected. A report I read in *USA Today* illustrated this most poignantly. Sandra Day O'Connor—the first female justice on the U.S. Supreme Court—retired in 2006 to care for her husband, John, who suffers from Alzheimer's. But this news item reported that John has "fallen in love with another woman at the facility where he lives," and quotes the O'Connors' son Scott as saying, "For Mom to visit when he's happy—visiting with his girlfriend, sitting on the porch swing holding hands"—is "a relief" to her.[54]

The report quoted a doctor as saying that although the disease takes away many abilities, the need for relationships doesn't go away. He commends the Justice for publicly disclosing this painful turn of events.

After all, five million families in the U.S. are living through the ravages of Alzheimer's. Opening the dialogue in the public square can help build camaraderie among them—and a greater understanding among those who want to support and encourage them.

Closing **Prayer**

God, I can understand why Job said, "What I dreaded has happened to me. I have no peace, no quietness; I have no rest, but only turmoil" (Job 3:25–26). I ask for Your grace in handling this unwanted trial. I ask for Your patience in caring for my beloved dementia patient.

Take *Action*

1. Turn to the Bible stories of Job, David (as he poured out his heart in the Psalms), and Paul (especially 2 Corinthians 12:7–10). As you see your emotions played out in their lives, journal your observations and make them your prayers to God.

2. Talk with your parent's doctor about finding a social worker who can see that you're trained to assist your parent.

3. Visit the websites listed on page 265 regarding elder-care services and dementia-care helps. Then enroll your parent in services that will provide you respite.

4. Talk openly with family members and friends about your challenges, and solicit help in a regular rotation of caregiving duties.

Chapter Twenty-One

I'LL TAKE
Senior Finances for $200, Alex

Making sense of financial

decisions related to aging

Alice Enters the New World of Her Mom's Finances

Three years ago, my mom told my sister and me that she didn't want to spend another winter alone in her Indiana farmhouse. That's when we decided to move her to an assisted-living apartment near my home in Colorado.

I felt bad moving Mom away from the town she'd lived in so long. But I looked into options there—and it was more expensive for less care than we could get her here. The assisted-living apartment she'd have to move into there wasn't at all appealing.

Mom gave me power of attorney, so I took over her finances while my sister coordinated the packing, handled the changes of insurance and prescription drug plans [Medicare Plan D], and sent out the change-of-address cards.

My role in charge of Mom's finances initiated me into a new world. I'd never been involved with Social Security and Medicare. The tax *implications for her were crazy. She has farm rental income in Indiana. Her accountant in Indiana lets me know each year how much tax she should be paying there and how much in Colorado. I have to trust he is calculating this properly.*

Just to figure out her assets—how much the farmland and savings bonds were worth—was a huge task, but you have to figure that to get her into a facility. The accountant sent me a worksheet that helped.

One of the biggest stresses was to figure out how much care she could afford. How long is she going to live? Will it be too long to stay in the nicer place for the rest of her life? There are different tiers of assisted living and a big difference between the tiers. I had to learn how to trust God for her finances. The farm has been in the family for six generations; we may have to sell it, because her bills are only going to go up.

Right now, it's not so bad, because I got into a routine and know what needs to be paid each month. I discovered computer bill-pay, which helps. And I made up a chart of income and expenses each month.

My sister has been an amazing partner, and our mother hasn't fought us. But I already felt I was at maximum before Mom moved here. I had to let my workload drop (and thus my income), but within a few weeks of moving, Mom told me, "I feel better than I've felt in a long time." That made it all worth it.

TWO YEARS AGO, MY DAD began wanting to talk to Mom and me about family expenses and income. He would bring up the subject at the most inopportune times—like when I was on deadline or when Mom and I were packing for a business trip. But he seemed to be feeling an increasing urgency for us to know where to find all the information we might need.

It's not that I don't want to know; it's that I don't want to know—yet. My motto has been, "I will look at no document before its time."

The other day, though, I took a glance at his yellow legal pad, flooded with penciled-in numbers, narrow columns, and microscopic footnotes. (How many times have I created Excel spreadsheets for him?) After my instant migraine began to subside and the numbers stopped swimming behind my eye sockets, I found a new respect for Dad. Beginning the transfer of responsibility for a lifetime of finances before it's medically necessary takes foresight and trust. I found myself humbled by the fact that he'd confide in me this information he's cared for painstakingly.

Everyday Financial Issues

But not every patriarch or matriarch has as much foresight as my dad. Often, an adult child asking financial questions of a parent feels like the Prodigal Son, asking for his portion of the family's inheritance to squander for personal gain. But if that fear keeps us from asking the right questions when we have the opportunity, we might pay the consequences later.

A *Family Circle* article stated the obvious: "Money is a touchy subject for many families, but as a potential caregiver you need to know where your parents keep their financial documents. If they ever become unable to manage their own affairs, you may need to access their financial resources in order to pay their bills."[55] The article listed eight questions adult children need to ask our parents. Number four was, "Where do you keep your financial papers?" The writer included a suggested wording to help parents understand what we need to know, and why:

Reassure your parents that you don't need to know their assets. Just where they keep the important information. Encourage them to list their Social Security and Medicare info; sources of income, including pension, investments, and interest; bank account numbers; credit card numbers; insurance policies; the location of any safe deposit boxes; and any debts in one file.[56]

That list isn't comprehensive, but it's a great start. Some of it overlaps with documents you'd need to check your parent into the hospital, so it is doubly useful.

Additionally, financial experts advise us to talk with our parents about signing power of attorney documents, to allow them to designate a financial decision maker ahead of a crisis. This person will be able to sign documents and pay bills for a disabled parent. It could be crucial in keeping insurance policies, house payments, and utility bills current.

Choosing for Your Parent

Public relations executive Olivia assumed responsibility for her mom's finances because "Her memory loss was affecting her ability to make sense of bank statements." Olivia, who has her mom's power of attorney, set up her mom's checking account so her mom can still cash small checks. But Olivia balances the account, pays her mother's bills, and makes financial decisions in her mother's best interests. "I try to be a good steward of what's available."

Olivia says she and her siblings, along with their mother, came to the conclusion that, because one day she may require long-term care, it was time for her to begin disbursing her assets. Because they'd earned her trust over many years, their mother agreed to a gradual relinquishment of her money to them.

Olivia says that although official ownership transferred, she and her brothers keep those funds separate—for use only in their mother's care. "Mom is seeing that we are continuing to care for her in exactly the same way now as we did before money changed hands." She keeps records of her mother's income and expenses scrupulously, so if her brothers ever want to see them, they'll be clear and easy to understand.

It's not easy or fun taking over this role—but like Alice, Olivia has found it one necessary adjustment—in a line of many.

Private Insurance and Government Provision

Before all the terms in the world of senior adult finance have you feeling like a *Jeopardy* contestant unable to ring in with one correct answer in the category, it might help to have a brief overview of a few financial issues before older adults.

Government Health Insurance

"Medicare is our country's health insurance program for people age 65 or older. . . . The program helps with the cost of health care, but it does not cover all medical expenses or the cost of most long-term care."[57] This government program, while not perfect or comprehensive, does cover senior citizens with a measure of health insurance.

For those in poverty situations, another government program, Medicaid, fills in some gaps. For example, if a senior outlives his savings but requires costly care, Medicaid will see to his care. However, the "tier" of care, as Alice put it, may be significantly lower than private care.

Private Health Insurance

Where Medicare covers a portion of medical bills, private insurance can pick up some of the slack. It may be offered at a discounted rate from former employers or unions. Able-bodied seniors who don't have retiree insurance may work part-time for employers who offer health insurance. A more expensive option is enrolling in an individual Medicare supplement health plan with a private company, much like a self-employed younger adult would do.

Veteran's Coverage

For information on medical benefits available to veterans, visit the Veteran's Administration website: www.va.gov.

Prescription Coverage

With prescription drug insurance, there are private and public options. Some employers offer retirees prescription benefits, but beginning January 1, 2006, Medicare began offering every senior prescription coverage under its Plan D. A booklet I picked up at a local pharmacy advised seniors: "If the drug plan you have is at least as good as Medicare, you can keep what you have. If your current drug coverage is not as good, think about joining a Medicare drug plan." The benefit of the Medicare plan is, "Your income, the state of your health, or the cost of your drugs will not matter."[58]

Long-term Care Insurance

According to a glossary of terms on John Hancock Insurance's website, "Long term care insurance . . . helps defray the costs of assistance with the activities of daily living or the costs of supervision due to a severe cognitive impairment and allows you to receive the type of care you need in the setting that's right for you."[59]

There are conflicting opinions about whether long-term care insurance makes sense for senior adults (because their premiums are so high). I consulted with two financial advisers—one heartily recommended this insurance for absolutely everyone; the other said it's a waste of money. What I do know is: according to *Genworth Financial's 2007 Cost of Care Survey* (pages 1–2) the average monthly cost for a one-bedroom assisted-living unit is $2714.38 and the average annual cost for a private room in a nursing home is $74,806.

The most solid piece of advice I found in a MetLife brochure:

"Before you purchase a policy, be sure you understand exactly what is and is not covered. If you need help making a decision, consult a financial planner or adviser. There are suitability guidelines developed by the National Association of Insurance Commissioners [www.naic.org] to help you determine whether a policy is right for you."

Local Government Subsidies

Caregiving son Dean discovered local government assistance programs in preparing his new home for his disabled mother. Where his mother had been receiving rent assistance before moving in with him, she was able to continue receiving the same amount after moving into an in-law apartment in his home. Another local program paid to install a lift on the stairs between her apartment and the main living space, so she can move around freely.

Costs to the Caregiver

Even if your parent is self-supporting through Social Security income, retirement benefits, and investments, you may incur expenses related to her care. As Alice, a small-business owner, found, she can't carry the client load she'd had before. Her household misses those lost wages—even though she's working harder now than ever, in an unpaid position as her mother's keeper. This is typical for caregivers.

As women know, the balancing act eventually begins to tip. To continue providing care for those they love, many women find they must take time off from work, pass up transfers, reject promotions or retire early. This can place added strain on themselves, their families, and their finances.[60]

Wills and Trusts

There is one other major category of information related to elder finances: estate planning. We'll address this in greater detail in the next chapter, but here, one principle that applies to financial decisions is in order. First, let's define terms. According to the MetLife Estate Planning pamphlet,

> Successful estate planning transfers your assets to your beneficiaries quickly and with minimal tax consequences. Estate planning can also assure that family members know how you'd like your financial and medical affairs to be handled if you become incapable of making your own decisions. The process of estate planning includes inventorying your assets; talking over important decisions with family members; and making a will and/or establishing a trust.

But even here, the decisions transcend the financial—and wind up squarely in the spiritual realm. According to financial adviser Ron Blue, "The process of wealth transfer is essentially a spiritual experience. It is not merely a financial or legal matter. You have to work it out in the presence of God and to His glory. What a marvelous privilege God has granted us to select His next stewards." Because of the spiritual weight of these decisions, Blue says, "[I recommend] the use of a lawyer specializing in estates and trusts. Involve your certified public accountant and financial adviser."[61] And whom does Blue recommend? Someone who shares your values and beliefs. If you have a biblical worldview, he advises you find advisers who come from that worldview.

Where the Treasure Lies

Ron's comments lead to the crux of the financial decisions we may help our parents make (or make for them). He sees financial decisions as part of our stewardship—our responsibility for assets God temporarily entrusts to us.

This is a principle initiated by Jesus, when He challenged His followers to "store up for yourselves treasures in heaven. . . . For where your treasure is, there your heart will be also" (Matthew 6:20–21). Keeping our parents' assets for their use in times of crisis would align with this biblical concept. Being more concerned with their well-being than with inheriting a large estate would align, as well, as would being willing to set aside our earning power so we can provide personal care to our parents.

In short, it's a matter of a change in perspective—realigning our definition of *treasure* to fit Jesus' definition. Think of Peter's challenge: "Praise be to the God and Father of our Lord Jesus Christ! In his great mercy he has given us . . . an inheritance that can never perish, spoil or fade—kept in heaven for you" (1 Peter 1:3–4).

How does this look in the real world? Frances's mother-in-law designated Frances to administer her estate finances. When the time came to disburse it all, Frances observed a difference between her husband's two siblings. His sister was concerned with getting all their mother's bills paid before disbursing the estate. But his brother was anxious—to the point of insistence—to get his hands on his portion of the money. Because Frances and her husband treasure family harmony more than any corruptible inheritance, they divided the estate three ways, gave the brother his third, and paid the remaining expenses out of their and their sister's portions.

Closing **Prayer**

God, again I'm overwhelmed with the financial decisions I may need to make for my parent. Help me discern how to be a good steward of the goods You've entrusted to my parent. Impart to me Your wisdom in sorting through the counsel of advisers—and lead me to those who would help me honor my parent and You.

Take *Action*

1. Help your parent create a list of critical financial documents. Be sure someone in the family knows where to find this list.

2. Encourage your parent to consult a financial adviser so his wishes are carried out.

3. Discuss signing a financial/legal power of attorney to allow someone she trusts to make these decisions for her.

4. Do Web research on financial issues related to aging so you'll ask the right questions of advisers. Start with: www.benefitscheckup.org; www.naic.org; www.kingdomadvisers.org; www.medicare.gov; and www.socialsecurity.gov.

Chapter Twenty-Two

KNOW ANY
Good Lawyer Jokes?

An overview of legal

issues involved in aging

All For One—Frances's Family Makes a Joint Decision

When my mom had to be hospitalized late in her lung cancer illness, a hospital social worker met with our family to fill out paperwork. One of the first things they asked was whether Mom had a DNR [do not resuscitate] order or a living will. We didn't have either. It wasn't something we'd felt ready to consider. But Mom knew she was dying—and it was obvious we needed to consider it at that moment.

The social worker explained that both of these documents would allow Mom to make her wishes known regarding the last days of her terminal illness. With Mom's input we decided the living will would be a good idea for her. She designated which of us would make medical decisions for her when she couldn't make them for herself and what her desires were.

We explained it to Dad—now, that was a tough discussion. In the end Dad decided to sign a living will himself, even though he was healthy. It came in handy a few years later when he was hospitalized. He'd made *his preferences known, and we were able to act intelligently and decisively based on what we knew he wanted.*

While we were going through this with Mom and Dad, my sister, her husband, my husband, and I came to the conclusion that we needed to sign our own living wills. At first, my brother-in-law wasn't keen on the idea. But as we talked, he became less squeamish. The social worker provided forms that are legally binding in our state, and we made our choices.

My husband and I have two daughters, and we decided to split the decision-making responsibilities between them. We assigned our attorney daughter as our financial power of attorney and our executor. She has the expertise and willingness to serve well in this role. Our younger daughter we assigned as our medical decision maker. She is compassionate and doesn't make quick judgments. That's what we want in someone making medical decisions when we can't make them for ourselves.

We keep these documents—legally signed and witnessed—at our house. It doesn't do any good to keep them in a safe-deposit box—or anywhere else where we can't get to them quickly.

They told us it would be good to give one copy to our family doctor, have one on file in the hospital, and keep one with us. I never filed them with our doctor or hospital, though, because doctors change, and we have several hospitals in our area. For us, it works keeping them close at hand, ready to grab, just in case.

I'M NOT A LAWYER—I don't even play one on TV. In fact, my three milliseconds as a pre-law major as a college freshman sent me away with little more than a nervous stomach. All I know to do when faced with legal issues like those associated with my Gram's and parents' aging challenges is to call a trustworthy attorney who specializes in the area of my immediate need—whether estate planning, property law, or end-of-life decision making.

That said, the best I can offer in this chapter is an introduction to a few terms to be familiar with when seeking legal counsel. As I move through these terms, I'll introduce stories of families who have grappled with these issues in real-life drama.

As you read, know that legal issues regarding aging vary widely by state and as legislatures pass new laws. In fact, these laws change frequently, requiring a periodic review of even the best-prepared documents to be sure they'll stand up to current law.

Olivia found this true when she moved her mom across state lines:

> My mom had a living trust she'd had an attorney prepare for her while she was teaching school. But when she moved in with me, I wanted to make sure it lined up with Illinois law. I took it to an attorney familiar with estate taxes and inheritance laws in Illinois and asked her to review everything. I'm grateful that Mom was open to that—because it could have been messy if it had not been cared for. There were some things Illinois requires that she didn't have in her documents, so our attorney provided the forms for Mom to fill out. Now it's complete and tucked away safely.

Asking the Right Questions

But sticky financial issues are just the beginning. The more emotionally charged issues are related to end-of-life choices like those Frances's family faced. While we'll consider the ethical dimension of end-of-life dignity in the next chapter, there are a few legal issues to consider now.

The first is being sure our parents' legal choices are made while they are coherent and able to sign documents legally, being of "sound mind," as the old line goes. Once dementia or another mind-debilitating situation has gripped a parent, it's too late to sign a document or ask his wishes. In the absence of signed documents, state laws govern who makes the decisions and by what standards they're made. How could the state—or even the most qualified medical professional—

provide adequate direction regarding what our parent would want done (or not done) on his behalf?

Knowing this, in her article in *Family Circle* magazine titled "8 Questions To Ask Your Parents" Winnie Yu writes, "While it's not easy to discuss your parents' wishes for the future, it may be one of the most important talks you'll ever have." Yu's number three question is, "What do you want me to do when you can't make your own decisions about your health?"[62] It has to be asked—and if a parent isn't the first to bring it up, it's our role to do so.

Nurse Jeanette Giambolvo tells of an elderly woman patient her team fought to save a number of years ago:

She was dying, and we were working our tails off to save her. The day she turned the corner, I was with her. She was angry; she told me she wanted to die. I remember telling her, "There is so much to live for."

"Like what?"

"The sun is shining; it is a gorgeous day outside."

She frowned and said, "Now I just have to go through that process of dying all over again."

I remember thinking, Sometimes the best intentions aren't good enough. Her wishes should have been made clear to us before she came in.

Today we are much more sure. No one should present at the hospital without a copy of those instructions [living will, medical power of attorney, DNR forms]. Unless I have a copy of those instructions on file, I have to do whatever is possible to save a life. My best counsel is to keep these instructions in your wallet.

Willing to Serve

From a parent's perspective, making the choices and making them known to the family are only part of the issue. The other is finding out whether designated decision makers are willing to serve.

The division of tasks Frances and her husband established between their two daughters does more than acknowledge each daughter's strengths or equally distribute the burden between them. It allows the daughters to weigh in on the responsibilities chosen for them. Both girls have agreed to serve their respective roles. But what if one had preferred not to?

That is the case with Marie. She makes day-to-day medical decisions, dispenses medications, and attends appointments with her dad's doctors. But she doesn't want life-and-death responsibility. "My brother handles the medical power of attorney—I don't want to handle that. He knows what Dad wants. Dad has signed off on end-of-life issues." While Marie knows her brother will act according to their father's wishes, she's not sure she could make the tough calls. It's commendable that she'd feel free to decline to do what makes her uncomfortable.

Documents, Terms, and Their Functions

Those are the big-picture parameters. But you're probably thinking it's past time to define the terms I've been using. Gram's life insurance agent provided me with an *Estate Planning* booklet prepared by MetLife that helped me begin making sense of them. It explains:

> Good planning dictates that you have two powers of attorney—
> one for financial matters, and another to deal with medical issues; you can, if you choose, select the same agent to perform
> both duties. You are not giving up your right to act in your own
> behalf; you are ensuring that your agent will be able to act
> when and how you have directed, if it becomes necessary. Also,
> it's important to note that you can revoke, or cancel, a power of
> attorney at any time.

According to these definitions, a **power of attorney for property** designates a trusted person to handle financial affairs when the signer is incapacitated. This can include paying bills, handling bank accounts, even selling assets to pay for long-term care or other expenses.

Conversely, a **power of attorney for health care** assigns a trusted person to make medical (not financial) decisions in the signer's place.

Additionally, there is a document called a **living will** (aka an **advance directive**). According to www.caringinfo.org, "A living will allows you to document your wishes concerning medical treatments at the end of life."

The MetLife booklet explains, "A living will . . . allows you to specify the kind of treatment you want in specific situations." So where the power of attorney for health care names a person to act on the signer's behalf, the living will lays out the signer's wishes.

Dr. Vicki Rackner, writing in a press release after the much-publicized Terri Schiavo end-of-life medical case, explains why both the power of attorney for health care and the living will are crucial:

> When you enter the medical system, your job as a patient is to make choices. The process, called informed consent, involves weighing the risks and benefits of one intervention and comparing it with alternatives. While these are called medical choices, they are really personal choices, reflecting your values, preferences and spiritual beliefs. That's why, according to US law, medical ethics and common decency, you as the patient are the one who chooses.
>
> You always have the option of choosing no treatment at all. Our law states that a competent adult has the right to refuse treatment even if it means that he or she will die without it.
>
> One day you may not be in a position to make choices for yourself. The medical and legal systems have provided mechanisms to guide the decisions you would make for yourself—if you could.[63]

In addition to these, Frances used one other acronym; Jeanette alluded to it, as well: a **Do Not Resuscitate** order **(DNR)**. This is a legal form—specific to your state—that a patient and his doctor can sign if a terminally ill patient chooses to keep anyone from performing CPR to revive him when his heart stops. The form gives legally binding direction to medics and others—and must be readily accessible, should the need for it arise.

Advance Planning

There are some resources available to help us prepare to meet an attorney about both medical choices and the distribution of estates. An initial consultation may net a worksheet to help us assemble all the information to prepare the documents we are seeking.

Crown Financial Ministries, a Christian organization with roots in the late Larry Burkett's Christian Financial Concepts, offers a free Christian will planning kit, downloadable from its website, www.crown. org. According to Crown, "Your will empowers you to specify how your assets are to be distributed when you die. Second, your will offers you the opportunity to leave behind bequests and declarations that affirm your relationship with Christ." The kit is designed to help a family think through all these issues before meeting with a professional.

In addition to a will, there are various options for trusts that provide alternative ways to pass estates down without invoking probate. An attorney's services are crucial in making these choices depending on a family's financial state.

Trustworthy and Willing

Financial advisor Ron Blue says all the legal issues associated with aging parents are built on one foundation: "They are based on a trust relationship between parent and child. There are biblical principles of responsibility [that come into play]." Trust is at the heart of every good legal relationship—from choosing an attorney to designating a power of attorney to selecting an estate executor. It's a topic the wisdom literature of Scripture is vocal about. Consider these proverbs (both from the NKJV):

Proverbs 19:20–21: Listen to counsel and receive instruction, that you may be wise in your latter days. There are many plans in a man's heart, nevertheless the Lord's counsel—that will stand.

Proverbs 1:5: A wise man will hear and increase learning, and a man of understanding will attain wise counsel.

As we mentioned last chapter, Ron's counsel is, "I recommend talking to a Christian attorney" who, he says, will be able to balance biblical principles like trustworthiness, accountability, and honoring God's counsel with legal and financial concerns.

Again, trust is pivotal. When I wrote *Staying True in a World of Lies*, I spent a big chunk of my page count considering trustworthiness. Here's how I defined it:

Every institution in our civilization is built on some element of trust. . . . Any definition of *trust* contains an element of truthfulness. Their root is the same. We cannot trust without truth; only pure, unadulterated truth earns our trust.

Mercifully, trustworthiness is a character trait God exhibits in abundance. Says the Psalmist, "The statutes of the Lord are trustworthy" (Psalm 19:7); says the ancient Hebrew king, David, "O Sovereign Lord, you are God! Your words are trustworthy" (2 Samuel 7:28); says the New Testament apostle Paul, "The Lord's mercy is trustworthy" (1 Corinthians 7:25). No matter what degree of trust we can (or can't) place in those around us, we can always trust God to be and do what He says.[64]

So, as we are thrust into positions of proving our trustworthiness to our parents, it's encouraging to know that we have an amazing role model in God—to show us the path and offer the wisdom we'll need that can only come from above.

Closing **Prayer**

God, I'm not comfortable raising end-of-life and financial issues, but I know it's important that I do. Please give me opportunity to raise the topic and give my parent willingness to share her wishes. Give us wisdom, that we'll please You in all the choices we make regarding the end of my parent's life.

Take *Action*

1. After prayerful consideration, gently open a discussion with your parent about his wishes regarding end-of-life decisions.

2. Seek legal counsel to get your own and your parent's estate plans in order. Two sources for finding elder-law attorneys are: American Academy of Estate Planning Attorneys: www.aaepa.com; and National Academy of Elder Law Attorneys: www.naela.com. Also, try www.findlegalhelp.org.

3. Visit www.caringinfo.org/AdvanceDirectives to search for a state-specific living will or medical power of attorney.

4. For information on acting as a medical power of attorney, visit: www.caringinfo.org/PlanningAhead/AdvanceDirectives/ChoosingHealthcareAgents.htm.

Chapter Twenty-Three

NO ONE CARED
for Me . . . Like Hospice

Helping a parent live fully until death

Lois Watkins: Hospice Volunteer

While I was pastoring, various people of our church were in hospice, and I was often there with them when hospice was attending to their needs. Also, my mom had cancer thirteen years ago, and we had firsthand, positive experience with hospice.

Hospice bathed Mom. They gave us rest. They gave us relief. When Mom died, they were the first ones to call—and they stayed with us while we waited for the funeral director.

When we moved, I felt a need to be in a meaningful ministry. A friend in church is a volunteer coordinator for hospice. We got talking, and he hooked me in. Of any volunteer work, hospice is the one I would have chosen. One of my strengths is compassionately helping people through really difficult times. There is not much that is more difficult than watching a loved one die. As a person gets sicker, there is a sense of not being as valued. I have a heart to value those not valued.

My role as a hospice volunteer varies. Tomorrow night I am going on respite care. The husband is a caregiver, and he is going to his granddaughter's basketball game. I am going to sit with his wife. Earlier this week a family caregiver became ill, so three volunteers sat with the patient while the caregiver went to the doctor. Other times I'll be there to give respite by talking with families and patients as they are able. One lady I visit in a nursing home has a bird feeder outside her window; I go out and put feed in it. Most often I read Scripture with them or sing with them.

When they are closer to dying I have opportunities to minister to families, to answer questions, to help them know what is to be expected. Hospice is good about giving people a sense that this is normal, to be expected, so they don't "freak out." In essence, hospice is valuing life until the person is actually gone.

Volunteers go through twenty to thirty hours of classroom training—with different aspects like the signs of dying, grief, and legal parts of it. We end up knowing more about death than any person has to know.

You don't get used to it like a doctor or funeral director does. It does take its toll. Last summer my favorite patient died, a couple of others I didn't know as well died, and a couple of personal friends died—all within six weeks. There are those you get closer to. With some families I have become friends and have maintained contact after their loved one's death.

I READ IT AT MY GRANDMOTHER'S bedside in the waning moments of her life as my voice choked and my throat constricted: a familiar Scripture believers have read at countless bedsides—to give comfort to the dying and the sorrowing. But something about it makes me shudder: "Yea, though I walk through the valley of the shadow of death, I will fear no evil: for thou art with me" (Psalm 23:4 KJV).

The valley of the shadow of death. It's a valley I wish I never had to enter again. If you've watched a loved one die, you know it isn't a sweet-smelling meadow of green grasses and gentle breezes. It's arctic winter: howling, bone-chilling, shiver-inducing. It's mountain walls crushing in. It's darkness-shrouded ravines and craggy stumbling stones.

Yes, for the believer in Christ, God stands on the other side of the valley, offering open-armed entrance into paradise. Therein lies the comfort. But traversing that brutal valley made Jesus weep and sweat drops of blood, and it's not a place I'd choose to camp out long. That's why I hold in high esteem folks like Lois, who choose to walk that foreboding valley with families as hospice staff and volunteers.

Lois says, "I'm hopeful that Christians and churches will be more equipped and willing to walk with patients and families through the valley of the shadow of death. Of any people, we should have a view of death that allows us to face it and comfort others."

Living until We Die

Hospice pioneer Dame Cicely Saunders said, "You matter to the last moment of your life, and we will do all we can, not only to help you die peacefully, but to live until you die." It's the line between living and dying that becomes a problem. Many biblical issues come into play when considering death and dying in the twenty-first century. Because modern medicine, with all its marvels, exists in the gray area between preserving life and delaying death.

There is the one extreme, played out eerily in Oregon, where 1998 saw the implementation of the Oregon Death with Dignity Act—which, according to the sponsor's website, allows "dying patients to control their own end-of-life care." It is, in essence, the legalization of physician-assisted suicide—where patients whose doctors certify that they have six months or less to live can obtain a prescription for and self-administer a lethal dose of drugs. According to the Oregon Department of Human Services, by "the end of 2005, 246 Oregon patients used the law to hasten their deaths."[65] On the other end of the spectrum is the unprecedented ability of the medical profession to delay death using chemicals and equipment that can either allow a patient's body time to recover—or more often hold her in suspension between life and death.

When we arrived in ICU with Gram, Mom and I were barraged with "what-if" questions from the medical team. *What if* her blood pressure drops? Shall we initiate a special IV to artificially sustain her blood pressure? *What if* her breathing becomes labored? Shall we place her on a ventilator? *What if* she "codes"? Shall we resuscitate her? To their credit, this young team of physicians was anxious to do everything possible to sustain Gram's life. Yet, there she lay, her mind sharp and attentive—her body obviously dying, writhing in pain and inconsolable. "I want to go *home!*" she kept crying. We knew *home* wasn't her condo.

We faced a problematic decision, because we are convinced of the inherent value of God-given life. We considered Jesus' words about the value of the individual: "Are not five sparrows sold for two pennies? Yet not one of them is forgotten by God. Indeed, the very hairs of your head are all numbered. Don't be afraid; you are worth more than many sparrows" (Luke 12:6–7). Only literally days before, I'd interviewed Pastor Colin about these issues—not foreseeing our need for biblical perspective in such short order. As we walked in the shadow of death that night, his words echoed in my mind:

> *There is a huge difference between sustaining a life that God is taking and taking a life that God is sustaining.* Sometimes knowing where the line lies can be horrendously difficult. As a pastor it is important for me to say they are two different things. Knowing the line exists is of huge importance. Medicine is not called to be in the position of sustaining a life God is taking. [A family needs] to find peace in knowing there is a time when a machine is to be turned off. Our task before the Lord in any given situation is to discern clearly where that line lies.

Using this counsel—and our earlier conversations with Gram where she opposed the idea of being placed on a ventilator—Mom and I chose to allow the special IV line to be inserted in an attempt to sustain Gram's blood pressure, but we stopped short of authorizing a ventilator. Because everything happened so fast, hospice wasn't called in—and we felt very much alone in this decision.

Once we made the call not to artificially sustain her life any longer, the team administered a pain drug (like hospice might in slower-unfolding circumstances) that freed Gram's body from pain. Later we watched her vital signs dwindle. We prayed; I read the Twenty-Third Psalm; and Mom and I sang to her—"Precious Lord, take my hand/Lead me home." At the moment of the last note of the song, her vitals zeroed out—and she was home. We found this a confirmation to us that we'd rightly stopped fighting against the events God had set in motion. We felt the reassurance of Jesus' words to His followers as He faced His death: "I have told you these things, so that in me you may have peace. In this world you will have trouble. But take heart! I have overcome the world" (John 16:33).

What Hospice Is and Isn't

For those with days', weeks', or months' warnings of a loved one's impending death, hospice can provide trained medical and emotional support for the walk through death's valley. Remember Dame Saunders's statement about a patient living peacefully until he dies. Hospice isn't about advancing death—like the Oregon law allows. It's about enhancing quality of life as it winds down from years to moments.

According to www.ElderLawAnswers.com, "Hospice programs emphasize relieving pain and managing symptoms rather than undertaking curative procedures." The site lists typical hospice services for the dying as including:

* nursing services

* doctors' services

* drugs, including outpatient drugs for pain relief and symptom management

* physical, occupational, and speech-language therapy

* home health aides and homemaker services

* medical social services

* medical supplies

* short-term inpatient care including respite care, procedures necessary for pain control, and acute and chronic symptom management

* training and counseling for the patient and family members

Lois clarifies the roles of each hospice team member. "On each patient's hospice team is a doctor who sees the patient and does monthly reviews with the team. The nurses take care of the hands-on things medically—prescriptions and the like. Also on the team are a chaplain, social worker, and volunteers."

All these services can help bring the issues Mom and I faced in ICU to the forefront before a loved one is in her final crisis. By definition, those who have been recommended for hospice by their physicians are no longer seeking "curative" care—medical care like chemotherapy to attempt to cure disease. Instead, they are receiving pain relief and symptom management—to help them live as comfortably and alertly as possible until the end.

Following a physician's suggestion to enroll loved ones in hospice (despite its lingering stigma) isn't at heart giving up on them—it is instead providing them with as much quality of life in dying as their deteriorating conditions allow.

Hospice Testimonials

Often families who have received help from hospice are enthusiastic but unable to articulate the tangible benefits they received. They'll say, "I don't know what we would have done without hospice"; or "Those people from hospice cared for our mother/father/whole family." In a time of such intense emotion, specific scenes give way to a general blur of one day morphing into the next.

It's challenging for caregivers to stop to gain perspective. Hospice workers, like other home health-care professionals, see things we miss. For Marcy, hospice was a godsend. "We had hospice for a whole summer before Mom died," she says. "It was the hospice nurse who recommended we place Mom in nursing care." Again, hospice saw what the family couldn't (or wouldn't). Where Marcy was concerned about a promise she'd made to her mom, hospice professionals were more objective and could identify the fact that Marcy's mom needed twenty-four-hour medical care.

Frances, whose mother was served by hospice in the last days of her battle with lung cancer, saw another benefit to the compassionate hospice professionals:

> Hospice could get the doctors to call back right away. This was a better response than we were getting from Mom's other medical team. A change happened when Mom became terminal. Maybe it's that the doctors felt like they'd failed her. Whatever it was, they were reluctant to call back once they knew there was nothing else they could do to cure her. But when we needed a change in prescription or a doctor's counsel, hospice nurses were able to get that quickly.

According to social worker Kim Jensen, many doctors used to be hesitant to sign a patient into hospice, in part for the reason Frances identified—they felt they were giving up and failing their patients.

But this doesn't always serve a patient well. Kim says hospice works best for those who still have a few months (rather than hours or days) of life expectancy. This is because it can help a family prepare emotionally, spiritually, and physically. And hospice can be available 24/7/365.

Not Just for the Dying

One additional benefit warrants mention: hospice isn't just for the dying. It's also for caregivers—offering support groups, respite care, and grief support. Hospice grief groups are free and usually open to the community—whether or not a loved one died under hospice care. Lois says this service makes hospice a useful tool for a family's processing of grief. She calls it "aftercare bereavement counseling" and speaks highly of its work.

A Legacy of Faith

While hospice does not make dying patients talk about death and dying, it does open the door to conversation with those ready to discuss the topic. Willing to acknowledge his mortality in hospice care, a mature patient can consider and pass on a legacy to his family that has more value than dollars and sense.

We see a pattern for this in 1 Kings 2. King David prepares for his impending death by giving a charge to his son and successor, Solomon, to keep the faith and continue in God's righteousness. Commentator Matthew Henry observed, "He feels himself declining, and is not backward to own it, nor afraid to hear or speak of dying."

The Nelson Study Bible continues: "David was following spiritual precedent as well as the custom of the ancient Middle East by passing on instruction to his son (see 1 Chronicles 28; 29). David's charge to Solomon was reminiscent of Moses' words to the Israelites (Deuteronomy 31:6)."

Apart from the physical respite and compassionate, skilled care from hospice, perhaps the greatest benefit can be the opportunity to walk through the valley of the shadow of death, eyes wide open, and prepared for eternal life that awaits.

Closing **Prayer**

God, please help me—and help our caring team—to prepare my parent for the walk into eternity. When the time comes to make end-of-life decisions, give us Your Spirit of wisdom and discernment and willing ears to hear Your loving direction.

Take *Action*

1. If your parent has received a terminal diagnosis, talk openly with her and her medical team about whether hospice is an option.

2. Before signing with a hospice group (even one recommended by a trusted doctor), research what different hospices offer. One might offer a "tweaked" program that could be better for you.

3. If your parent is in hospice, consider using inpatient respite that can allow you a short time off or even one good night's sleep.

4. Avail yourself of hospice respite, bereavement counseling, and support groups.

Chapter Twenty-Four

THERE'S GOT
to Be a
Mourning After

Owning and experiencing

the grief of parting

Julie Observes Another's Grief

I received a call that a family friend who'd experienced a series of strokes over the course of the last several years had gone home to heaven. He'd been cared for lovingly by his wife and children through all the challenges of his illness; they'd sacrificed much to be with him 24/7. His widow asked that a ladies trio I'm in sing for his funeral service.

A week ago Saturday, I joined my two friends and sang at the service that celebrated this godly man's life, testifying to his love for family and church—and honoring the God he spent a lifetime serving. The family wept. And we all wept together over the loss—the fact that, as one of the members of the trio put it, "We'll never relate with him just the same way again. The next time we'll see him will be in heaven—and everything will be different. Good, different. But different."

The next day, I joined the other members of the trio and my mom as we became the worship team for the Sunday service in the sanctuary *where we'd shared that meaningful memorial. We began the service with upbeat music. I felt a little funny as I saw the grieving family file in to line two whole pews. Here we were celebrating Jesus with vivacity, and there they were red-eyed.*

After a Scripture reading, we slowed the pace and experienced a meaningful worship moment. Right in the middle, the pastor stopped to invite anyone who would like to come to the altar to pray. He looked at the worship team and said, "Ladies, sing something." On the fly, we chose a few songs, including, "I Love You, Lord," figuring it would be simple for the congregation to pick up in case the PowerPoint operator couldn't locate the slide. We sang it a few times, then dropped out as the piano played on.

Just then we heard a clear soprano voice from the congregation ring out with great conviction, "I Love You, Lord, and I lift my voice to worship You . . . " Always curious, I opened my eyes to see who was singing with gusto—and there she was, the new widow, tears streaming down her face, arms outstretched, lifting her whole being in worship.

I won't soon forget her statement of faith in that moment—she was the flesh-and-blood depiction of the scriptural truth, "We don't grieve as people who have no hope." She may have lost her love on earth, her husband of more than fifty years—but she didn't lose her first love, Jesus Christ, whom they'd served together.

WHEN I GAVE THE SALVATION MESSAGE at Gram's funeral service, I was surprised that while my voice choked up a time or two, I didn't "lose it" completely. I experienced what I can only describe as a supernatural strength of voice and focus of mind that allowed me to speak God's truth with clarity and conviction.

One of my cousins commented to her father that she wondered how I was able to do it—and he told me he responded, "Julie can do it because she really believes what she's telling you." I'd have added that I want everyone else to believe it, too.

Perhaps that's why my heart connected with the widow singing, "I Love You, Lord." I recognized in her the same Spirit who had equipped me for my task—as He was now equipping her to give testimony before her family of God's nearness in our grief.

That's the subject we'll address now, as we conclude our examination of the issues of caregiving. Mom thought I should title this chapter "Good Grief." But instead, I chose "There's Got to Be a Mourning After," in acknowledgment of the fact that the challenges of caregiving don't come to an abrupt end the moment our loved one is freed from suffering. Rather, our processing of all we've endured and all we've given up has just begun. The mourning—like the morning—must come after our caregiving responsibilities draw to a close.

Expressing Grief in the Early Going

After Gram died, the hospital chaplain gave Mom and me a pamphlet (Advocate Lutheran General Hospital, "Grief and Growth") on what we could expect next. It read, "Grief is learning to say 'goodbye.' Without exception, this means pain. The intensity of pain will vary depending on the circumstances and the relationship with the deceased, but it will generally affect your entire being."

We'd grieved before, so we knew the drill—shock, denial, anger, sadness, frustration, and eventually acceptance. But each time we go through the process, the emotions—and their expressions—are slightly different.

According to grief counselor Alan D. Wolfelt, "Especially if you had little or no opportunity to anticipate the death, you may feel dazed and stunned now and in the coming days. Trust that these feelings are normal and necessary. They serve as psychological 'shock absorbers,' giving your emotions time to catch up with what your mind has been told. You may also find yourself crying (or laughing) hysterically, having angry outbursts or simply feeling foggy and unable to think. These are common feelings" (from the Dignity Memorial Brochure, "Helping Yourself at Your Time of Loss").

When death freed Marcy's mom from dementia and cancer,

Marcy says, "I was mentally numb and exhausted. I couldn't cry until later, when I could process it all." In addition, she experienced a gnawing guilt in feeling relief that the episode was over for her, as well as her mother.

According to hospice volunteer Lois Watkins, guilt is a typical emotion for adult children who have watched a parent die. "Feeling guilt in feeling relief is normal," Lois says. "Family dysfunctions escalate at these times, so I try to smooth things out for the family. I answer questions, helping them know what to expect."

Expressing Grief While Handling the Mundane Details

Unfortunately, in this moment of emotional mayhem we who are left behind feeling numb-angry-sad-lost are called on to make myriad decisions and deal with countless details—everything from choosing a funeral director, to picking out a casket and flowers, to arranging for those who will participate in a service.

Something is going to fall through the cracks. For us, it was my fault. I carefully picked out all Gram's clothes—down to her foundations—but alas, when we got to the funeral home, I realized I'd forgotten shoes. The funeral director said not to worry—that no one would see her feet. But I felt guilty sending Gram to burial shoeless.

This experience with a compassionate funeral director illustrates the importance of choosing the right funeral director. Even before a parent nears death, it is helpful to ask friends, extended family, or church leaders for referrals.

The church my grandfather pastored built a wonderful relationship with a funeral director in Chicago. We knew him to be honest and to treat church members with dignity. When he died, his son and daughter, Joe and Ginny Lucania, took over with the same ethic as their father. There is no guilt, no high-pressure sales pitch from Joe and Ginny, no "If you really loved your mother, you'd spend more money on [casket, flowers, grave marker]."

For years, Mom carried Joe and Ginny's number in her planner. One of the first calls she made from the hospital's bereavement room was to them—and Joe answered the phone. Mom started to cry when she realized a lifelong friend would help us make Gram's final arrangements. There they were, unexpected tears, the first of many we'd experience. They were tears of relief that we weren't alone.

In a spiritual sense, we knew we weren't alone. We clung to the reassuring truth that death made Jesus cry (John 11:35), and that He collects our tears in a bottle (Psalm 56:8 KJV). But it helped to have friends with professional expertise to be "God-with-skin" to us.

And they didn't offer only expertise in the arrangements. Because they are part of an association of funeral homes, they were able to offer more. Your local director may also offer some of the following:

Travel Discounts. Our extended family still lives in Chicagoland, but one of the services the association provides is help obtaining bereavement travel discounts to allow far-flung family to attend a funeral.

Bereavement Counseling. Another benefit is twelve months of bereavement counseling, similar to that from hospice, churches, and community organizations.

Notifying Businesses/Government Agencies. Joe provided an *Aftercare Planner,* to help us begin notifying Social Security, insurance companies, utility companies, and the condo homeowner's association of Gram's death. The package contained sample letters, checklists, a CD-ROM, and a warning list of scams that prey on the grieving.

It says, "There are financial institutions, organizations, companies, government agencies, and personal contacts that must be notified to help prevent identify fraud. Information and documents must be gathered and estate matters addressed. Benefit claims, household accounts, and changes in business relationships must be handled."

While we were experiencing the lack of focus that the hospital grief brochure warned us to anticipate, this notebook provided us with something concrete to do—and an orderly, organized way to accomplish a task for which we were ill prepared. Other funeral directors have similar packages, so it would be worthwhile to check with your director for materials he or she can provide to help with the immediate business details.

Expressing Grief with Trusted Loved Ones

Part of the rationale behind holding a funeral or memorial service is to give others an opportunity to remember our loved one and to come alongside us in our grief. Mom, Dad, and I were grateful for the nearly two hundred friends and family who came to pay respects to Gram. They were a comfort to us—in their presence, their gift of time spent with us, and their loving arms surrounding us. We got to hear stories of how she'd impacted others' lives—and to reminisce about our memories.

But when we got home, I was ready to get alone, but Mom and Dad wanted to talk about all we'd just heard—who had come, what they'd said, how nice it was to see them. Which illustrates the fact that some want to have others with them around the clock until they adjust to a new normalcy. Others prefer to do much of their grieving in private.

Dr. Wofelt gives this counsel: "If having others around comforts you, ask them to stay. If you need some alone time, tell them so and ask them to come back tomorrow." The danger is in isolating ourselves. His counsel gives us license to be silent or numb or angry or chatty. Whatever works for us. As long as we remain connected to an inner circle.

Expressing Grief with a Savior Who Understands

Remaining connected to our Savior is perhaps the most pivotal issue as we process our grief in healthy ways. Pastor and author Dr. David Jeremiah offers these words of hope:

With a heart smashed in ten thousand pieces, you have no clue where to turn. How wonderful, then, is the moment when you discover you can run into the arms of a Father who loves you and weeps with you. He is not a God who dwells in some distant, unapproachable realm, who paid a short call on this planet centuries ago—but . . . He is an always present Father, who is totally immersed in the smallest details of our lives.[66]

That word picture of a child running to the waiting arms of a loving Father—and looking up into His eyes to find that what makes us cry makes Him cry—is a biblically accurate portrayal of God. Listen to Revelation 21:4–5:

And God will wipe away every tear from their eyes; there shall be no more death, nor sorrow, nor crying. There shall be no more pain, for the former things have passed away. Then He who sat on the throne said, "Behold, I make all things new." And He said to me, "Write, for these words are true and faithful." (NKJV)

Whether we are introverts or extroverts in processing grief, the reality of our loving Father taking His hand to wipe away every tear we've shed and to banish death and sorrow forever is the living hope that can keep us going throughout our caregiving journey—from its early onset through its ultimate conclusion.

This knowledge can equip us to do some remarkable things. It can allow an only granddaughter to give a funeral message without choking up. It can allow a grieving widow to sing out the words to a love song to Jesus. And it can allow a pastor/son to give a stirring tribute about his mother to his congregation.

Let me tell you about that. In the same service with the grieving widow, we had a grieving pastor whose mother had been on hospice care and had died from cancer fifteen hours before. He changed his planned message and presented a sermon based on the apostle Paul's words, "For to me, to live is Christ and to die is gain" (Philippians 1:21). He told of his mother's conversion to faith in Christ as an adult and of how she had lived out her faith as a scholar and an eager witness the remainder of her life. In giving this tribute of one who had lived for Christ and died to gain eternal life, Pastor Tom found an outlet for his grief and a vivid challenge to his congregation.

Similarly, the church I attend regularly offered those who don't have the benefit of the pulpit an opportunity to give tribute to their loved ones. Before Christmas they held a Holiday Remembrance service. They opened it to the community, saying, "We hope it can be a time of healing and of sharing God's love."

Since taking our grief to Jesus is always right—as these believers illustrate—let's close by reading some of the most hopeful words penned by the apostle Paul. They're found in 1 Corinthians 15:51–58, and I'm quoting from the *New Living Translation*, because in this translation, they're so vivid:

> But let me reveal to you a wonderful secret. We will not all die, but we will all be transformed! It will happen in a moment, in the blink of an eye, when the last trumpet is blown. For when the trumpet sounds, those who have died will be raised to live forever. And we who are living will also be transformed. . . . Then, when our dying bodies have been transformed into bodies that will never die, this Scripture will be fulfilled: "Death is swallowed up in victory. O death, where is your victory? O death, where is your sting?" . . . But thank God! He gives us victory over sin and death through our Lord Jesus Christ. So, my dear brothers and sisters, be strong and immovable. Always work enthusiastically for the Lord, for you know that nothing you do for the Lord is ever useless.

"Nothing you do for the Lord is ever useless." Not your selfless caregiving. Not your being sandwiched between demands of your household and your parent's needs. Not your end-of-life choices. Not your handling of your parent's funeral. Not your handling of the financial and legal and medical details. None of it is beyond the Lord's notice—and none of it is beyond becoming part of His plan for your ultimate good and His glory.

So, exhausted, overwhelmed caregiver, hold on to that truth no matter where you are along the caregiving road. "Whatever you do in word or deed, do all in the name of the Lord Jesus" (Colossians 3:17 NKJV), for "nothing you do for the Lord is ever useless."

Closing **Prayer**

God, while I know my grief is nothing that isn't common to every person, it's bigger than life in my view right now. Let me feel Your arms around me. Let me sense You are catching my tears—and will one day wipe them away. For now, surround me with friends who can help me adjust to a new stage of life—post-caregiving. Thank You for being with me through the journey. Even in my grief, may I bring You glory. Amen.

Take *Action*

1. Visit the Federal Trade Commission website to obtain a funeral planning checklist: www.ftc.gov/bcp/conline/pubs/ services/funeral.htm

2. Get a copy of David Jeremiah's book *A Bend in the Road: Experiencing God When Your World Caves In* (Thomas Nelson, 2000) to find biblical answers to your deepest questions.

3. Be open with a few trusted friends about your grief, asking for help in areas where you feel most vulnerable.

4. Consider how you'd like to be remembered—and make an effort to work enthusiastically for the Lord so your life will one day be another example of Philippians 1:21: "to live is Christ and to die is gain."

APPENDIX 1
Key Quotes from Experts on Aging

On the Pervasiveness of Family Caregiving

U.S. Surgeon General Carmona: "Forty-six million Americans are providing uncompensated care for an adult family member or loved one who is chronically ill or disabled, often sacrificing career advancement, personal pleasures, and their own health and well-being out of a combined sense of love and duty."

On Healthy Aging

Nurse Jeanette Giambolvo: "Today, it's not unusual for me to have a patient who is more than 100 years old. They may be ninety and still driving (which can be more than a little scary), or 100 and still riding a bicycle. . . . They're not just living long, but many are having a high-quality life well into their later decades."

Dr. Judy Salerno, National Institute on Aging: "Disease and disability are not inevitable consequences of aging. . . . Maintaining good habits and positive attitudes is what we should all be aiming for."

Healthguide: "Most vital organs gradually become less efficient with age. . . . An active body that gets plenty of oxygen, water, and nutrients is more likely to function efficiently for a longer period of time."

Psychologist Jennifer Thomas: "I encourage families with a relative who has lost some independence to help them maintain an ability to serve others, because that's a critical part of living."

On Loss in Aging

Psychologist Alice Domar: "In a way, someone who is aging has lost someone: they have lost the person they once were. They are likely to be grieving the loss of their ability to do the things they used to do." [www.strengthforcaring.com; "Understanding Our Loved One's Emotions as They Age"]

Psychologist Jennifer Thomas: "Get them in touch with old friends who remember their shared history. They'll remember your parents and tell old stories together."

On Bringing Up Difficult Subjects

Dr. Carol Anderson: "When talking with your aging parents, it's important to use an approach that lets Mom or Dad know that you want to understand him or her better and that you are not trying to take over his or her life."

Winnie Yu in *Family Circle*: "Money is a touchy subject for many families, but as a potential caregiver you need to know where your parents keep their financial documents. If they ever become unable to manage their own affairs, you may need to access their financial resources in order to pay their bills."

On Going to the Doctor

National Institutes of Health: "Making a list of your symptoms before your visit will help you not forget to tell the doctor anything. Your list should include:

 ❊ what the symptom is
 ❊ when it started

* what time of day it happens and how long it lasts
* how often it happens
* anything that makes it worse or better
* anything it prevents you from doing."

On Estate Planning

MetLife: "Successful estate planning transfers your assets to your beneficiaries quickly and with minimal tax consequences. Estate planning can also assure that family members know how you'd like your financial and medical affairs to be handled if you become incapable of making your own decisions. The process of estate planning includes inventorying your assets; talking over important decisions with family members; and making a will and/or establishing a trust."

On Being a Patient Advocate

Vicki Rackner, M.D.: A patient advocate "promotes the best interests of the patient. A family caregiver can serve as an advocate and help a friend or relative take the fastest, most direct course from illness to optimal health. It does not require specialized medical training. . . . Be sure to get permission to step into the patient advocacy role."

On When to Visit the ER

American College of Emergency Physicians: Visit the ER when experiencing any of the following:

* Difficulty breathing, shortness of breath
* Chest or upper abdominal pain or pressure
* Fainting, sudden dizziness, weakness
* Changes in vision
* Confusion or changes in mental status
* Any sudden or severe pain

* Uncontrolled bleeding
* Severe or persistent vomiting or diarrhea
* Coughing or vomiting blood
* Suicidal feelings
* Difficulty speaking
* Shortness of breath
* Unusual abdominal pain

On Negotiating Family Disagreements

Ron Blue: "It's best to have all the affected people in the room together. . . . It can be a difficult situation—a lot of people cannot deal with it emotionally. In these cases, you may get a facilitator, a financial planner or accountant who has done it before . . . someone who can integrate biblical wisdom into the advice and counsel."

Psychologist Jennifer Thomas: "Few things are more powerful in human relationships than learning to accept responsibility for failures and to sincerely apologize to the person we have wronged."

On God's Supernatural Strength

Pastor Colin Smith: What you would expect in a bad relationship would be bitterness, complete alienation, or even hatred. That is natural. But the Holy Spirit of God gives us something better than that. He enables us to overcome bitterness. In later life for an adult child to serve and minister to the very people who abused him or her—that can only be attributed to God's grace at work in the person of the Holy Spirit."

On Memory Loss

Dana Alliance for Brain Initiatives: "Occasional forgetfulness is a perfectly normal part of life. Certain types of memory slips, such as forgetting names or where we parked the car, are common even among the young. In fact, in young and old alike, stress, sleep problems, certain prescription medicines, and depression are associated with memory difficulties. On the other hand, memory problems that significantly impair day-to-day functioning are cause for concern and should be evaluated by a qualified medical professional."

National Institute on Aging: "The term *dementia* describes a group of symptoms that are caused by changes in brain function. Dementia symptoms may include: asking the same questions repeatedly, becoming lost in familiar places, being unable to follow directions, getting disoriented about time, people, and places, and neglecting personal safety, hygiene, and nutrition."

On Sharing Faith with Aging Parents

Pastor Colin Smith: "Be careful in watching for the clear opportunity to speak, be sparing about that; avoid the snare of always speaking. And be very sure that we work on the beauty of our lives as believers. That will open the door for greater receptivity at the moment of speaking."

On How the Church Can Help

Pastor Colin Smith: "A care team [from the church] offers guidance, the ability to pray, a place to talk, even brings meals. The church is a natural extension of family—relationships within the life of the church should reflect family in a healthy way."

Arlene Allen, director of women's ministries, Assemblies of God: "Nursing-home ministry or shut-in ministry can be more of a blessing to the giver than to those to whom we go to visit. I used to take my young preschool son with me when going to the nursing home, because they loved to see small children. 'Can I hold him?' I was often asked. He was comfortable with the attention, and they always invited him to come back."

On Nursing–Home Care

Aging Parents and Elder Care: "Nursing homes provide care for people whose medical needs require the attention of licensed nurses, but not the more intensive care of a hospital. Admission requires a doctor's order. Nurse's aides provide much of the day-to-day care. Social workers and case managers help seniors and their families with insurance issues and the coordination of nursing care plans. Dietitians, physical and occupational therapists and other health professionals help support and sustain seniors' physical and emotional well-being."

Myziva.net: "You can speak with the hospital discharge planner, who can suggest several nursing homes that may meet your needs. Elder care lawyers, your doctor, clergy, ombudsman, the Department of Social Services and your local library can be very helpful."

Experts, cited on www.myziva.net, suggest residents bring only:

* Clothing that is comfortable and does not require dry cleaning and preserves the resident's dignity and right to choice in what he/she wears
* Photographs and memorabilia
* Personal effects such as makeup and hygiene products
* Eyeglasses, dentures, hearing aids, and prosthetic devices

On Legal Issues

MetLife: "Good planning dictates that you have two powers of attorney—one for financial matters, and another to deal with medical issues; you can, if you choose, select the same agent to perform both duties. . . . You are not giving up your right to act in your own behalf; you are ensuring that your agent will be able to act when and how you have directed, if it becomes necessary."

On End-of-life Issues

Dame Cicely Saunders, hospice pioneer: "You matter to the last moment of your life, and we will do all we can, not only to help you die peacefully, but to live until you die."

Pastor Colin Smith: "There is a huge difference between sustaining a life that God is taking and taking a life that God is sustaining. Sometimes knowing where the line lies can be horrendously difficult. As a pastor it is important for me to say they are two different things. Knowing the line exists is of huge importance. Medicine is not called to be in the position of sustaining a life God is taking. [A family needs] to find peace in knowing there is a time when a machine is to be turned off. Our task before the Lord in any given situation is to discern clearly where that line lies."

On Caregiver Self-care

Psychologist Jennifer Thomas: "Secure your [oxygen] mask first, before helping others around you secure theirs. You can't help your mom or dad if you have passed out yourself. . . . Caregivers need to take a break."

The Dana Alliance for Brain Initiatives: "In many cases, caregivers become isolated and lose touch with social contacts, which can worsen stress and have a negative impact on overall health. . . . Caregivers may experience stress-induced health changes that may increase the risk of heart disease or cancer in susceptible individuals. A series of studies have linked the chronic stress of caregiving with impaired immune-system function, which makes the caregiver more susceptible to infectious conditions such as flus or colds, and may slow healing processes after an injury."

APPENDIX 2
Web and Print Resources for Caregivers

Books of Note for Caregivers

How to Care for Aging Parents by Virginia Morris, Workman, 2004.

Christian Caregiving—a Way of Life, Dr. Kenneth Haugk, Augsburg, 1984.

The 10 Greatest Struggles of Your Life, Colin S. Smith, Moody, 2006.

Splitting Heirs, Ron Blue and Jeremy White, Moody, 2004.

The Five Languages of Apology, Gary Chapman and Jennifer Thomas, Moody, 2006.

How You Can Be Sure That You Will Spend Eternity with God, Erwin Lutzer, Moody, 1996.

Dictionary of Eldercare Terminology—2nd Edition by Walter Feldesman, National Information Services Corporation, 2000.

He Cares New Testament, NLT, Tyndale, 2007.

Hard Choices for Loving People: CPR, Artificial Feeding, Comfort Care, and the Patient with a Life-threatening Illness, Hank Dunn, A & A Publishers, Inc., Herndon, Va.

Faith-based Organizations to Help Caregivers

Hopekeepers: www.hopekeepersmagazine.com

Stephen Ministries: www.stephenministries.org

Government Helps for Patients and Caregivers

Medicare: www.medicare.gov
Elder Care: www.eldercare.gov
Administration on Aging: www.aoa.dhhs.gov
National Council on Aging: www.ncoa.org
National Institute on Aging: www.nih.gov/nia
Department of Veterans Affairs: www.va.gov/

PERS: Personal Emergency Response Systems

Medic Alert: www.medicalert.org
Acadian On Call: www.acadian.com
Easy Living Lifeline Program: www.easylivingprogram.com
Medical Alert Systems: www.seniorsafety.com
ADT Home Health Security Services: www.adt.com

Caregiver Associations and Support

National Alliance for Caregiving: www.caregiving.org
National Family Caregivers Association: www.nfcacares.org,
  www.thefamilycaregiver.org
National Organization for Empowering Caregivers: www.nofec.org
Care-givers: www.care-givers.com
Caregiver Magazine: www.Caregivermag.com
Rest Ministries: www.Restministries.org
Children of Aging Parents: www.caps4caregivers.org
Aging Parents and Elder Care: www.aging-parents-and-elder-care.com
Family Caregiving 101: www.familycaregiving101.org
AARP Magazine: www.aarpmagazine.org/caregiving
Strength for Caring: www.strengthforcaring.com

Medical Resources

Most illnesses or diseases have foundations or associations. Use your Web browser to locate the site with more information on your parent's health issue (such as the American Diabetes Association [www.diabetes.org], American Heart Association [www.americanheart.org], Alzheimer's Foundation [www.alz.org], American Cancer Society [www.cancer.org], American Stroke Association [www.strokeassociation.org], etc.).

Personal Health Care Passport: www.kahnhealthcare.com

Medical History Organizer: www.Sotellmeorganizer.com

National Rehabilitation Information Center: www.naric.com

Medications for the Needy: www.needymeds.com

Pharmaceutical Assistance: www.rxhope.com

Patient Advocate Foundation: www.patientadvocate.org

American Health Care Association: www.ahca.org

National Association of Professional Geriatric Care Managers:
www.caremanager.org

Mayo Clinic: www.mayoclinic.com

Web MD: www.webmd.com

Improving the Doctor-patient Relationship:
www.medicalbridges.com

Dementia-care Helps

Alzheimer's Foundation (including Safe Return Program):
www.alz.org

The Alzheimer's Store (gadgets to make life easier):
www.alzstore.com

Alzheimer's Disease Education and Referral Center:
www.alzheimers.org

National Institute of Neurological Disorders and Stroke:
www.ninds.nih.gov

Dana Alliance for Brain Initiatives: www.dana.org

Selecting a Professional Counselor or Psychologist

Your state psychology board will list licensed psychologists in your area.

Focus on the Family: www.family.org or 1-800-a-family
American Association of Christian Counselors: www.aacc.net
National Mental Health Association: www.nmha.org

Nursing Home and Assisted Living Decisions

The Complete Nursing Home Guide: www.MyZiva.Net
Consumer Consortium on Assisted Living: www.ccal.org
Center for Excellence in Assisted Living: www.theceal.org
My Guide for Seniors: www.myguideforseniors.com

In-home Care and Safety

National Resource Center on Supportive Housing and Home Modification: www.homemods.org
Patient Advocate Foundation: www.patientadvocate.org
Private Duty Home Care Association: www.pdhca.org/missions.html
HomeCare Physicians: www.homecarephysicians.org
National Association of Home Care for/and Hospice: www.nahc.org
American Academy Home Care Physicians: www.aahcp.org
Accreditation Shield (formerly Home Caregivers Accreditation of America): www.shieldaccreditation.com
Home Instead Senior Care: www.homeinstead.com
Active and Able Product Catalog: www.activeandable.com

Hospice Care

Patient Advocate Foundation: www.patientadvocate.org
National Hospice and Palliative Care Organization: www.nhpco.org

Finding a Local Hospice: iweb.nhpco.org/iweb/Membership/MemberDirectorySearch.aspx?pageid=3257&showTitle=1

Home Care and Hospice Agency Locator: www.nahc.org/Agency Locator/

Hospice Chaplain/Author Hank Dunn: www.hardchoices.com

Financial and Legal Resources

National Association of Elder Law Attorneys: www.naela.org

Elder Law Answers: www.elderlawanswers.com/index.asp

Crown Financial Ministries: www.crown.org

Kingdom Advisers (Ron Blue): www.kingdomadvisers.org

American Bar Association:
www.abanet.org/lawyerlocator/searchaop.html

Financial Planning Association: www.fpanet.org/public/index.cfm

CarePlanner: www.careplanner.org/default.htm

Benefits CheckUp: www.benefitscheckup.com

Household Helps for the Overwhelmed Caregiver

Meal Preparation

Dream Dinners: www.dreamdinners.com

DineWise: www.dinewise.com

Let's Dish: www.letsdish.com

Super Suppers: www.supersuppers.com

Local Meals-on-Wheels Listings: www.MealCall.org

Grocery Delivery Service

(Availability of this service varies by region; try these sites or visit *www.local.com* to search for a grocery delivery service near you.)

Peapod: www.peapod.com

Netgrocer: www.netgrocer.com

WeGoShop: www.wegoshop.com

Simon Delivers: www.simondelivers.com

Safeway Stores: www.safeway.com

Part-time In-home Help

Helping Hands: www.lotsahelpinghands.com
Share the Care: www.sharethecare.org
Sitters for Seniors: www.care.com
Visiting Angels Living Assistance Services: www.visitingangels.com
Private Duty Homecare Association: www.pdhca.org/missions.html

Other Sites of Interest

American Medical Association Caregiver Self-assessment:
www.ama-assn.org/ama/pub/category/4642.html
United Way Information and Referral System: www.211.org
American Association of Retired Persons: www.aarp.org
Caregiver Expo: www.caregiverexpo.info
Dignity Memorial: www.dignitymemorial.com
Aging with Dignity: www.agingwithdignity.org
**National Resource Center on Supportive Housing and Home
Modification:** www.homemods.org

NOTES

1. www.medicalnewstoday.com.

2. http://www.nih.gov/news/WordonHealth/jun2002/successfulaging.htm.

3. Ibid.

4. http://12.42.224.225/library/healthguide/enus/illnessconditions/topic.asp?hwid=tn9719.

5. Ibid.

6. www.strengthforcaring.com; "Understanding Our Loved One's Emotions as They Age."

7. http://www.nih.gov/news/WordonHealth/jun2002/successfulaging.htm; "Keys to Successful Aging: Good Habits and Positive Attitudes" by Carla Garnett.

8. Dr. Carol Anderson, "Talking Points," http://www.strengthforcaring.com/manual/28/95/talking-points.html.

9. http://nihseniorhealth.gov/talkingwithyourdoctor.toc.html.

10. Ibid.

11. http://www.medicalbridges.com/newsletter_may_2007_1.html.

12. Ibid.

13. http://www.acep.org/patients.aspx?LinkIdentifier=id&id=26018&fid=1320&Mo=No&acepTitle=When%20Should%20I%20Go%20to%20the%20Emergency%20Department?

14. http://www.strengthforcaring.com/manual/stress-relief-communicating/understanding-our-loved-ones-emotions-as-they-age.html.

15. *US News and World Report*, Nov. 27, 2006, 61–66.

16. *Chicago CAREgiver*, March/April 2007, 19.

17. *Outreach*, July/August 2007, 110–12.

18. MarketWatch.com: 2007-10-25 07:12:08.

19. Christine Larsen, "Finding a Good Home," *US News & World Report*, Nov. 27, 2006, 64.

20. *Woman's Study Bible,* "Grandparenthood: Ministry of Love" (Nashville: Thomas Nelson, 1995), 932.

21. http://www.medicalnewstoday.com/medicalnews.php?newsid=57316.

22. http://www.aging-parents-and-elder-care.com/Pages/Checklists/Nursing_ Home.html.

23. Ibid.

24. http://www.strengthforcaring.com/manual/balancing-work-and-family-family/juggling-and-coping-skills-for-sandwich-generation-caregivers/.

25. Julie-Allyson Ieron, *Conquering the Time Factor: Twelve Myths That Steal Life's Precious Moments* (Camp Hill, PA: Christian Publications, 2002), 79.

26. http://www.strengthforcaring.com/manual/balancing-work-and-family-family/helping-the-kids-feel-important/.

27. http://www.strengthforcaring.com/manual/balancing-work-and-family-family/stuck-in-the-middle/.

28. http://www.medicalnewstoday.com/.

29. http://www.strengthforcaring.com/articles/57208.phpmanual/stress-relief-time-management/defining-the-help-you-need/.

30. Virginia Morris, *How to Care for Aging Parents* (New York: Workman, 2004), 28.

31. Ibid., 23.

32. Julie-Allyson Ieron, *Staying True in a World of Lies* (Camp Hill, PA: Christian Publications, 2001), 76–77.

33. http://www.strengthforcaring.com/manual/28/139/communicating-with-an-elderly-loved-one.html.

34. http://www.strengthforcaring.com/manual/28/95/talking-points.html.

35. http://www.caregiving.com/support/html/driving.htm.

36. The Dana Alliance for Brain Initiatives, *Staying Sharp: Current Advances in Brain Research: Quality of Life,* 15–16.

37. *Chicago CAREgiver,* Fall 2007, 26.

38. http://www.strengthforcaring.com/manual/28/318/caring-for-someone-with-mental-illness.html.

39. http://www.stephenministries.org/stephenministry/default.cfm/931.

40. http://www.stephenministries.org/stephenministry/default.cfm/928.

41. Gary Chapman and Jennifer Thomas, *The Five Languages of Apology* (Chicago: Northfield, 2006), 163.

42. Jan Silvious, *Fool-Proofing Your Life* (Colorado Springs: Waterbrook, 1998), 210.

43. http://www.strengthforcaring.com/manual/28/299/understanding-our-loved-ones-emotions-as-they-age.html.

44. The Dana Alliance for Brain Initiatives, "Chronic Health Issues" booklet, 7–8.

45. Ibid.

46. *Mayo Clinic Embody Health*, November 2007, 4.

47. *CAREgiver* magazine, Fall 2007, 26–28.

48. Dr. Thomas is credentialed with the American Association of Christian Counselors (www.aacc.net), as well as with James Dobson's Focus on the Family organization.

49. The Dana Alliance for Brain Initiatives, "Answering Your Questions About Brain Research Q&A."

50. National Institute on Aging: AgePage; "Forgetfulness: It's Not Always What You Think," http://www.nia.nih.gov/HealthInformation/Publications/forget-fulness.htm.

51. Ibid.

52. Morris, *How to Care for Aging Parents*, 468.

53. Ibid., 483–84.

54. http://news.aol.com/story/_a/a-new-page-in-oconnors-love-story/2007111 3082409990001?ncid=NWS00010000000001; A New Page in O'Connors' Love Story; by Joan Biskupic, *USA Today*; Posted: 2007-11-13.

55. Winnie Yu, "8 Questions to Ask Your Parents," *Family Circle*, November 1, 2007, 136.

56. Ibid., 134.

57. Social Security Administration: Medicare booklet, 2, September 2007, SSA Publication No. 05-10043.

58. *Medicare Prescription Drug Coverage: What Does It Mean for You?*, Albertsons, Inc., 2005.

59. http://www.johnhancocklongtermcare.com/tools/tools_res.jsp?selection =tools_glossary&cid=johnhancock&selectstate=IL.

60. Genworth Financial: "Our Future, Ourselves: A Guide for Women and Their Advisors in Preparing for Long Term Care," August 2007, 3.

61. Ron Blue, *Splitting Heirs* (Chicago: Moody, 2004), 57, 174.

62. Winnie Yu, "8 Questions to Ask Your Parents," 130, 134.

63. http://medicalbridges.com/press-releases-schiavo.html.

64. Ieron, *Staying True in a World of Lies*, 47, 48.

65. www.deathwithdignity.org/historyfacts.

66. David Jeremiah, *A Bend in the Road* (Nashville: Thomas Nelson, 2000), 107–9.

JAMES O'DONNELL

LETTERS
for
LIZZIE

A STORY OF LOVE, FRIENDSHIP
AND A BATTLE FOR LIFE

ISBN: 978-1-881273-01-1

Having just made a cross-country move, Jim expected that his new assignment from God was to teach in a small college in Indiana. He wasn't prepared for the task of dealing with the onset of his wife's battle for her life. A far-flung prayer network began - with personal reflections on a painful, years-long ordeal of cancer and heart disease. This book is the compilation of those insights...on faith, illness, and healing. A special section gives advice on "how to think" and "what to do" when faced with life-threatening illness. A remarkable true story of a husband's love for his sick wife.

by James O'Donnell
Find it now at your favorite local or online bookstore.
Sign up for Moody Publishers' Book Club on our website.
www.MoodyPublishers.com